CAN YOU
HANDLE
REAL TALK

RONNIE FLETCHER

Author ReputationPress®
Creativity & Branding

Author Reputation Press LLC
45 Dan Road Suite 36
Canton MA 02021
www.authorreputationpress.com
Hotline: 1(800) 220-7660
Fax: 1(855) 752-6001

Ordering Information:
Quantity sales. Special discounts are available on quantity purchases by corporations, associations, an
others. For details, contact the publisher at the address above.

Printed in the United States of America.

ISBN-13: Softcover   978-1-952250-45-3
          eBook   978-1-952250-46-0

Library of Congress Control Number: 2020907282

Books By Ronnie Fletcher

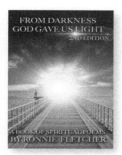

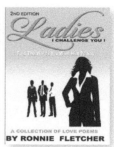

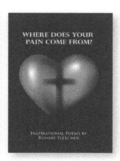

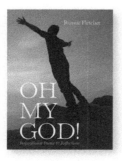

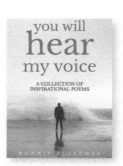

Your Stuff
And Someone Else's Happy Story

Today we heard a sermon that made everyone reflect about their own ways
We were startled by the words the preacher had to say
The question he posed made me think about my own life and God's glory
He asked the crowd the question, "What will be your story?"
We have money in our pockets, or it passes through our hands
That money we label ours isn't really owned by any woman or man
The Bishop stated money is simply a means to an end
If you feel money's grip, then cash money will be your only friend
The Lord blesses us with money to be a blessing and get what we need
Some people feel entitled, it's money that understands and targets your greed
Realize money is to complete GOD'S goals and help be His hands and feet
Or else you'll become greed's victim and be swallowed by its deceit
So many people live such a lonely life, rich but always worried about their cash
They distance themselves from everyone in fear they will take their stash
They buy so much stuff to show off to those who are without
Failing to find the joy in giving to those who have nothing but pain to shout
The person who can touch someone through the gift of giving
Will be filled with a new smile as they impact how someone else is living
Be generous with your money and bless someone that really doesn't have
You will feel the spirit of appreciation as their tears will be seen and felt throughout
Open your heart, open your mind, and spread the love to all
When the time comes for you to be with the Lord, it's your giving He shall recall
Give away your stored items, give away everything you no longer use or need
The time has come for you to realize you're blessed
And you have abused and missed opportunities to give
Imagine the faces that you can touch and provide a glimpse of God's special glory
Let this be the day you trade your stuff to create someone else's happy story

The Impact On A Child

Ladies and gentlemen, I need you to think back for awhile
What happened in your past may have a powerful impact on your inner child
We may never reveal the things that happened in our past
Some things are too painful to imagine, and we hope the thoughts don't last
There are triggers that may be set off in our minds
We try to forget those days, that life that was so unkind
Please be careful of the things you expose your children to
Some things are too traumatic and will impact what the grownup will do
That little child may wet the bed, or cry out in the middle of the night
When you respond or punish that child, they respond by saying, "I'm alright"
That terrible ordeal that was once or repeatedly witnessed by your child
Could be the true reason why anger has replaced a golden smile
Just know the memories of what happened through childhood never go away
As we grow to adulthood, we often question what made little Johnny or Susan this way
All children may seem harmless, cute, and some may even appear shy
Some grow to be adults and become fulltime menaces, you'll question why
Before you punish your child for something you should try to understand
What did they witness as a child before they became a woman or a man?
Pain comes from hurt and until it is dealt with, it will only repeat
Some deal with anger internally, while others take out their pain in the streets
We may never learn where it started or understand our child's pain at all
Just know that it's up to the parents to give them a foundation, otherwise they will fall
So, please mommy and daddy don't argue and fight just allow me to smile
Because what you say or do will have such an Impact on my inner child

Where Did We Go?

Last night while I was home alone
All I could do is wonder why you wouldn't call me on the telephone
Last night I asked the Lord, "Why?"
I questioned my heart about your love and that's when I began to cry
Do you remember how we would talk everything through?
You became my world and now I don't even know you
Each time I had a problem, you always seemed to have the right answer
Now I've become like a stranger to you, like I'm your cancer
I miss the connection that we once had
I can't help but think what could I have done for you to treat me so bad
Do you remember the nights we would talk until the sun would rise?
What happened to those moments, or was I just another door prize?
You once told me that I would always be able to trust in you
What happened to that person who now acts like I'm brand new?
Why have you become a stranger to the one who knew you best?
Do you recall when you said that you had no problem passing any one of my tests?
What happened to the person who said their love would always show and last?
Please answer, "Where did we go?" that is the question my heart wants to ask

Fellas, Why Do Ladies Stray?

Now fellas you know the reasons why the ladies stray
Most of you could be in denial, so I will tell you the facts today
Why do ladies stray from home yet keep their men around?
Let's look at what you really do when you're not putting the affection down
Do you pay attention to your ladies' conversations and her needs?
Do you only ask her what she likes when you want her to satisfy your own greed?
Your lady may love you and wants more of your time and affection
Have you lost touch with how you met, or have you gone in a new direction?
You may be a good provider and a great dad to your children
The question is how will you respond when her body asks where have you been?
You're the king of your household and you may have chosen her from a crowd
Now that she has become yours to love, what have you done to make her proud?
Sometimes a lady just wants company so she can share her day
How often have you talked or listened to what she really had to say?
Marriage or a relationship is still a joining of two hearts
Before you get involved, you need to think about what you're going to start
Some fellas just want sex without any commitments at all
This isn't a relationship, what you're really seeking is a booty call
Most women who have been hurt in their life seek their own way
They either want a relationship or just desire to run the streets and play
Fellas, you really need to think about things and put your cards on the table
Otherwise you'll be in a losing game, she'll stray since you weren't available or able

Family Can Hurt You!

Today is a good day because the Lord gave it to me
Sometimes I question the Lord's actions as to how he let this be
You try not to let anybody too close to your heart
Family is the one who can do the most damage from the start
We don't have any choice about who our family is
Yet, the pain family can inflict can push us to the edge
When you learn about family and they learn about you
Some members are so sweet while others always question what you do
Why does the family only gather for a party or a painful event?
Why do some bring happiness while others bring their drama with their vents?
As we grow older and begin to find our own way
We realize that tomorrow isn't promised so we need family every day
Each day that we wake up is another day we should reach out to a different member
Just to say hello and try to get back to the days of September
Every time there is a problem within the circle of your own family
There is usually a peacemaker who will say casually
"Let bygones be bygones and just let things be"
Sooner or later the troubled family member will be exposed and brought to their knee
When you inquire, "Why are they like that?" The real answer will never be known!
All you can do is shake your head when their cover is blown
Just remember to love your family no matter what they do
Please keep your friends close because it's your family that will hurt you.

My Wake-Up Call

Hello, my love can you please have a seat
Do you remember the time you said, "I make your heart weak?"
Hello, my heart, remember what you once told me?
You said, "You have captured my heart and it doesn't want to be free"
When we first met you seemed to know all the right words
As time went on, I realized you were just talking to the birds
When I looked into your eyes and fell in love at first sight
I tried to remain strong, but my heart felt something wasn't right
How many times did I say please just be honest we me?
You cheated, you lied, and refused to just let me be
Each time that I gave you the trust of my fragile heart
You disappointed me, just like you did from the very start
I forgave you, and you would simply hurt me again
It's sad how we have become enemies instead of best friends
So many people warned me, there were signs about the real you
I couldn't hear their warnings because my heart wouldn't let me see through
You captured my heart, you stole all my precious pride
You hurt my feelings to a point that I could no longer hide
Finally, the day came when you allowed me to slip and fall
That was the day I answered the phone … hello it's your wake-up call!

We Hold On

While we hope for a better tomorrow as we sleep through the night
Only the Lord knows what will happen as we press and fight our good fight
Whether we hope to win or accept our losses
How long will we tolerate the abuses that were not chosen?
Some things that happened to us in life was wrong, unfair and has left us frozen
We continue to fight in what seems like a losing battle
Until we hear a voice that says, "Hold on, that's enough! Don't unravel"
Each time we face a struggle against us we rise to fight
Asking how the struggle got so fierce and continued into the morning light
When we give our all, and fight our best fight
We find we get stronger realizing it was The Holy Spirit that kept us through the night
Not everyone will win, not everyone is willing to stand and fight
Just know that if we have Jesus we will live and make it through the dark plights
Every struggle is a season, and every season has its end
Don't ever lose faith without first remembering your true friend
Jesus is your friend; Jesus is the spirit that guides your heart, mind and feet
Let's stand tall through the hard times as we begin to do our part and piece
Everyone has a will to one day see the Lord's Heavenly Gate
We only know of the Lord; we know God's answer will be our fate
So, rise my friend and take the hand of a stranger
Remember your hand was guided through the days of hidden danger
While your fears were always heard in places your spirit didn't belong
The Lord sent His angels to remind you to simply hold on!

Their History

Hello ladies and gentlemen, we need to think things through
Before you get involved with a person who doesn't have a clue
You may meet Mr. Wonderful or the Finest Lady in the world
But did you ever consider the mask that is worn by every woman and man?
Have them take a seat at the table and conduct an interview
Before you move forward, analyze the information you gather and review
You will need to know where they are from and what their goals are
Be careful what you ask, because their answers may seem like a wrecking bar
You may see beauty but somewhere in there may be a beast
Did you observe their anger at any time or the devil waiting to begin his feast?
Why are you single and please tell me the real, whole truth?
Do you begin to move forward, or should I wait for the goodness of Ruth?
What are your intentions and please be honest with me today?
Let's mark down this conversation so we can fully remember what we've said
Yes, we have established a physical attraction and a common interest
So, let's be clear before we get to a level place where we will require a witness
What was your home life like when you were a child?
Did you grow up with your parents and do you remember if you had a smile?
When your parents fought, did you witness any type of abuse?
Did you move past that memory, or did you seek to use it as an excuse?
Before we travel down the road of establishing any type of meaningful relationship
We need to know our goals, our hopes, our desires, so we can enjoy a partnership
I write this letter so we can both be clear and there will be no mystery
I'm announcing my intentions, let's begin to create what will be known as "their history"

You Don't Realize What You Have

Today we heard a message that woke my spirit up
I watched people as they entered and gathered in our place of worship
The room filled up quickly, to capacity and overflow
The preacher observed how many people arrived to hear the words of Our Mighty King
That's when the bishop called out, "Please come in, sit down and settle in!"
The bishop continued by saying, "This message today isn't one to be fooled around with
Everyone here needs to stop asking the Lord for unimportant things
Because you don't understand the power of what you desire can bring
How often have you asked the Lord to give you something, and then another?
Never turning to observe the blessings or the need of your sister or your brother
How often did you look around seeking more and more for yourself each day?
Never observing what you already received without giving thanks in any way
Why do you cry out for more when you already have more than enough?
Do you ever look around your circle to observe any lack and or who has it rough?
Do you ever look in your closet wishing for so much more?
Think about what you are asking before your final wish leaves out the door!
Do you ever take the time to observe what you have been given?
How often did you give thanks while others questioned how you're living?
Think about all these questions and you will begin to understand
Once you pay attention to what you already have, then you will see God's hand and his plan"

Why Do Men Cheat?

Today this question is asked by most ladies of today
Most ladies don't feel they are loved so their men begin to stray
While women feel they are victims who are cheated on
How many ladies have a man who feels like he hears the same old song?
Do you remember the effort you made to get that man's attention?
Ladies, you still want high love and affection, yet you fail to mention?
That you are no longer that loving woman, full of fire without apprehension
Where's the desire, the passion and your surrender in the middle of the night?
Today you don't apply the same effort, and it seems you just would rather fight
Ladies, you knew when you were dating that he would desire all your loving
Now we are down the road and you forgot the desires you should be giving
Sex isn't the only part of any relationship, but it does play a part
When you turn your man down, the real question is why did you ever start?
Whether you have children or go to work every single day
You still have an obligation to make time and allow him to play
Ladies, if you just want a sex toy to come over when you have a need
Make your intentions clear so that he will know what he needs to feed
Call him up, or wake him up and allow him to enjoy you
This is the main reason a man will turn away to replace what you use to do
What you won't do in your bedroom will eventually be done in another
Sex, friendship, whatever will arrive in the form of a sister or a brother
Think about these words and it's time to decide what you really want
Because there are so many lonely ladies who would love your man to flaunt
Take notice to what you have and please stand on your own two feet
Otherwise you will learn the real reason as to why so many men cheat!

I See The Real You

Can we sit down and talk about what we should do
First and foremost, I have now seen the real you
When we first met you promised me the world
Now we are at a point that I no longer feel like your girl
When we first met, we talked about where we were headed
Now 5 years later, you don't trust me, and acting like you don't get it
We once talked about the things we would one day do
What happened to the girl who once cared and who could share until she was blue?
I think we need to take a closer look and review our union
Our loving beginning was enjoyable, but now there's nothing but confusion
Please understand this letter isn't only about my feelings about you
The time has come to focus on what we need to do
We need to focus on pressing forward, moving ahead
What was once a promising relationship has become a train wreck, enough said
Let's remain friends while we pursue our possibilities
I see the real you and don't want us to be filled with hostility
While this may be a sad moment, we need to face some facts
Let's ask ourselves where we are really going, and weigh the impact
Arguing, complaining, no longer enjoying each other's company is our reality
If you ask me, we should cherish our good times, not be remorseful in actuality
We've reached a point in this relationship that marks our finality
I'm not blaming you, please understand you are just not the one for me
Let's just take the next step and work toward just being friends so we can be
We tried to make this work, the sign is on the door, it's a tough pill but true
I have a new pair of eyeglasses called clarity and I see the real you!

Man-Up

"Man-up everyone," the LORD said so
Stop your crying and complaining or you may have to go
The Lord spoke out with his Angry Voice
People froze in their tracks, not able to rejoice
Man-up everyone while you can understand
His voice was so loud that it was heard throughout the land
So many people live for themselves and that will have to change
Gather yourselves together because this war will be a sign of my rage
Man-up today and get your affairs in order
Once the Lord comes to this land, it will be his enemies that he shall slaughter
Don't ask any questions, as he tells his followers to rise
The Lord is calling His warriors out for the ultimate demise
Man-up everyone, as you assemble just know there is a risk and some causalities
When you begin to feel the pressure from the power and wrath of THEE
Why does it take a war for everyone to come together and become "WE"?
Man-up to these facts because it's the LORD who determines what will be
Gather around everybody the ground is about to erupt
When you hear the trumpet sound off, I really hope you're ready to MAN-UP

How Dare You!

Take a moment, look around at all the things you've been given
Have you ever said thank you for the life that you are living?
Do you really think that it's because of luck, that you have it all?
When will you realize what you have was simply all GOD'S call?
You show off the gifts that the lord has provided for you
Not once reflecting or acknowledging how little you had to do with it all
Now let's think about all that you have ever earned
Tell me when the smoke clears away, what have you really learned?
So many people who are so rich think "It's all about me"
Then the Lord steps in to remind them that I AM THEE
So many people expect to have the world laid down at their feet
Then the LORD steps in to remind them of who they might meet
So many people walk around feeling like they are really entitled
Never giving the Lord any of their time because they are worshipping an idle
So many people will live only to regret their own actions
The Lord will get the glory as he claims, and he addresses your attractions
Sinners, remember the LORD as you continue to follow and yield to your distractions
When Judgment comes, the Lord will appear to ask about your actions
"How dare you! "will be his response, what will be your reaction?

The Lord Wants You Hungry!

My friends I need you to pay close attention
Because today there was a message that very few will mention
There is a rumor going around that says the Lord can't hear you
Do you fully understand why the Lord wants you hungry?
Our Father is a jealous GOD and you shouldn't make any mistake about that
While he provides all your needs, He makes sure you remember those facts
You will always have a need, you will always have desires
This is the Lord's way of having you wanting His help to fight Satan's fires
When do people call GOD's name, how often do we call on THEE?
When do people pray for help if not for their own emergency?
When does a man cry out if not from the hunger within for more?
The Lord knows a man's heart in his time of need, for GOD'S hand to close another door
That hunger they feel inside, is the Lord's hand working on the spirit that you try to hide.
People go about their business feeling like everything will be okay
So, the Lord sends his reminder of how he can control your entire day
When you're full, you simply stop seeking the Lord's helping hand or even look His way
So, the Lord sends His Spirit of hunger to make sure you understand
Hunger doesn't always mean a desire for food, but it is a need that is at hand
Until you understand the Lord, then it's your hunger he will feed
So, take a moment and acknowledge the actions of THEE
Until you do this, expect his angel to be dispatched, cause the Lord Wants You Hungry!

The Lord Will Make A Way

Please take a moment out of your busy day
Trust in the Lord when He states that He will make a way
When your doubt arrives because of your fear
How can you say you trust your GOD when it's the devil's voice that you hear?
When you are faced with things that you can't understand
Who do you turn to if you don't believe in GOD'S plan?
When you were awakened this morning did you know what you were going to face?
Did you hear the LORD'S voice when he commanded you to stay in your place?
Why did you run when you were told that only GOD can protect you?
How often will you allow doubt and fear to guide your actions and distract you?
When you cried out for help who answered your call?
Haven't you realized that Satan is only here to see you fall?
How many times did you try to make the DEVIL your new friend?
But the Lord has the power and His word can determine your end!
When you were pushed against the wall he came to your rescue and allowed you to mend
The Lord watches everything and he knows where you have been
The Lord knows the answer because he created everything
Take a moment and ask Satan, "What help can you ever bring?"
When you have problems and don't know which way to turn
Ask GOD for guidance and his help so you don't crash and burn
Listen to the Lord's answer when He responds by saying, "I GOT you"
Each time you lose your faith, your trust, and your belief don't forget He KEPT you
Just know it is the Lord's voice that says, "I will always make a way! I Will Never FORGET you."

When Will You Learn?

Each day we experience new troubles for the day
Never losing sight of the problems of yesterday
If we take a moment to reflect on our bad times
We'd realize the lessons learned from remembering our past crimes
Every time you fell short and called out for the Lord
Did the memory return of the moment you pulled through and caused you to applaud?
When He came to your rescue did you ever say, "Thank you?"
Or, were you one of those people who felt that it was something the Lord owed you?
When will you learn that your actions are a result of your past experiences?
Be careful cause it can have a great affect or impact your today and my friend that is seriou
When will you learn that tomorrow is only a dream that may not come true?
Do you realize that it's only GOD'S hands that have truly provided for you?
When will you learn that not everyone comes in your life for GOD'S reason?
Some may be to teach you a life lesson, while others may be for a season
When will you learn that so much energy is used when you hate?
What is accomplished when you are alone to face your own fate?
Everyone will have their own judgement day
Will you be ready to face Your Father, and have you thought about what you would say?
Can you honestly say you did all you could do to help another?
Will you lie to your Father's face and say I was there for my brother?
Can you seriously say you've shown the love that the Lord has shown you?
Will you stand before your Father and say sorry My Lord for what I didn't do?
The Lord provides opportunities, yet we seem to let them burn
The question the Lord will ask is, "When will you learn?"

The Lord Will Provide Your Needs

Now pull up a chair and please have a seat
This message has so much power that it might knock you off your feet
Think about your desires, think about what you feel you need
Are your desires just a reflection of your own greed?
Have your wants and desires become more than you can bear?
You continue to seek things that never seem to appear
Who did you call out to when your back was against the wall?
When times became so difficult it was only GOD'S name you could recall
You remembered His Name in your desperate time of need
Hoping He would answer your call and your wish with lightning speed
Do you remember your proud days when you didn't need anyone?
Think back to the times when all you did was smile to express you were having fun
Do you remember your selfish days when you looked down at another?
Forgot where you came from and turned your back on your own brother
The Lord saw your real heart and chose to take your happy times away
Time revealed that you needed a new lesson that day
One by one, the Lord changed your vision and your desires
Each time you sought a blessing, the Lord allowed you to face Satan's fires
The time had arrived for you to be broken so he could begin His repairs
When you called for the Lord's help, you heard his whisper say, "Life isn't always fair"
Why did you call on the Lord, was it out of your desperation?
Why did you wait until he took away the blessings to have consideration?
You needed to be broken so you could appreciate those things you took for granted
Think about the days that changed because of choices you didn't refuse and what you hunted
Today you have a new mouth that you must feed
Hopefully this lesson shines a light on your understanding that it's the Lord you need

Rescue Me

Today I met a lady who lived on the street
She offered herself to any man that her eyes would greet
When I refused her advances, she turned and began to walk away
Until I called out to her with a special offer for the day
Please little young lady, can I pay you for a moment of your time
Let me be clear, what I require of you isn't a crime
Tell me your price for one solid hour of your attention
With a smile on her face, she gave me a list that she failed to mention
The list that she presented was for some clothes and food to eat
She wanted help and support from any man she would meet
Finally, I informed her that I would give her what I could
Would she spend the time I requested so that I could reveal GOD'S plan to her?
She responded, "Why would you help me, why would a stranger provide for my needs?"
That's when I sat her down so I could explain my own task
Please young lady I need you to understand, some day you will do the same
Help a stranger, become someone's light, just remember to pay it forward that's God's delight
The joy that I receive will be from the smile placed on your face
When you give yourself to the Lord it will be the day you change your place
Even on your darkest day the Lord will always be your light
While I take today to bless you my new friend, hopefully you will give thanks tonight
Give thanks to the Lord because as you eat and drink it's all from THEE
That's when this nice young lady's spirit cried out, "Lord thank you for rescuing me!"

I'm Afraid

Listen closely because these words don't come easily
While I have faced so much in my life, I often wondered why me
Yet, the lord has a way of making anyone fade
Even the strongest of souls must admit when they are afraid
Most men feel like they are stronger than the entire world
But you best believe they can be broken down like any little boy or a girl
Life comes with a cost so make sure your debts get paid
Before you find an angry soul who will make you confess that you're afraid
Some will never admit these two frightening words if they can help it
But what most people don't realize is that fear is legit, and I have felt it
We are taught that there is nothing in life that you should ever fear
Yet, we still run and hide from the unknown that causes us to tear
The two words that come from the unknown are "I'm Afraid"
But if we trust in the Lord's promise, then we will all get paid
Why are we afraid? Why do we allow fear to consume everything?
When we relax and trust the Lord, that's the calm He will bring
So many people go to the hospital and trust the hands of a surgeon
They trust a man with a tool, yet they fear the LORD'S emergence
"I'm afraid" are the thoughts that may never be spoken
Did you ever pay your fare for life, have you submitted your token?
Let's think of all the times the Lord allowed your fears to fade
Yet, you never stopped feeling these two words .... "I'm afraid!"

Hey Cry Baby

Have you ever met someone who does nothing but cry?
Each time you cross their path, only to ask the question why
Have you ever known a person who does nothing but complain?
Their presence which you once enjoyed has now become such a pain
Some people stay away from these children who do nothing but wine
The only time they want you around is when they want you to hear their cries
If you ever ask them why they are always crying
Their response is always the same, "You don't know where I've been"
Let's unpack that statement and you will see where the excuses begin
I warn you those might be harsh words they may not want to hear
Hey cry baby, it's time for you to wipe your weeping eyes my dear
There is a world out there that doesn't care, and you are in for a big surprise
Hey cry baby, everyone around you has their own problems I can surmise
But you're so busy crying, you can't hear anyone else's trouble and that's no lie
Hey cry baby, let's take a moment to understand what your real complaint is about
When we review all your facts, they don't give you a real reason to pout
Let's take a moment to understand the problems you claim are all on you
Stop the drama, stop the complaining, so that we can look at what else you can do
Hey cry baby, the time has come for you to find a large mirror
The reflection may reveal the real problem might be you're the terror
Have you seen the problem person and please don't say maybe?
Open your eyes and focus on the mirror that reveals the real cry baby

Hello Stranger

Yesterday, while I was walking down the street
Everybody else passed you by, but you were the one I was meant to meet
Now please don't get me wrong, because I know you really don't know me
I observed your smile, it seemed like a very powerful electricity
I know we are strangers, so I will simply ask for a favor
Could you please give me a clue?
Hello stranger, I noticed how the sun shines with your smile
I was wondering are you available to join me so we can chat for a while?
Please don't take this the wrong way
Let's just act like two children in the park on this bright sunny day
Take a chance on me as we step away from this world
We can hold hands in the park like I was your man and you were my girl
Hello Stanger, I want to show you the world in one night
Let's find or create our own Disney Park as we dance into a new daylight
We can walk down the streets and laugh and let's get lost in our own smiles
What a lovely thought this could be as we remember how it is to be a child
Hello Stranger, wouldn't you rather be happy as we dream today?
Take a minute and ponder the thought before you answer in any way
Please think about this moment that you allowed a stranger in
I wonder how you'll answer, my hope is that we can begin
Hello stranger, it's up to you to give me a chance and let me in your heart
All I ask is that you give me a moment, so our love can really get a jumpstart!

Don't Be So Demanding

Wow, is the first expression that came to my mind
When I observed you for the very first time, I just went into my own rewind
This lady is so fine! I wonder would she even talk to me
So, I remained quiet, I needed to figure out a way to see if she was free
After a minute had passed, I decided to approach her with my first move
All the while wondering, if she was taken or if she would decide to approve
Finally, I approached her with a simple "HELLO"
That's when she smiled back, as her pretty eyes wouldn't let me go
Excited, afraid, and caution all came calling upon me
My next move became clear as I wondered how this all could be
We exchanged numbers and began to have a great conversation
That's when she asked the question, "What are your expectations?"
She went on with more questions that were aimed at me
She never gave me a chance to answer, before she announced she is free!
I'm single, I'm lonely but I've been through so very much
Then she asked my intentions, as she announced, "I hope it's not just sex!"
If that's all you are after she said, "You can leave out the door!"
She finally paused for a moment and said, "I'm sorry for not allowing you to speak
It's just that I've been through so much, but it's time to turn the other cheek"
That's when she repeated her first question by saying, "What would you like?"
At that moment my thoughts became clear that I needed to take a hike!
I was still captured, attracted, as I wanted to get to really understand
What she experienced in her past … cheated on, sexually abused and just hurt by another man
I said, "I'm so sorry about what happened to you
Let's take this friendship nice and slow because I want to get to know more about you"
That's when she smiled, and hugged me as she announced, "I need a lot of understanding
She thanked me and said, "Your patience is required, and I ask that you don't be so demanding

I'm Adopted

Today I heard a story about a little boy
While he played every day, his life really had no joy
This young boy was teased in every way
The other children would talk about him every single day
The other children would always tease him about his circumstance
Never did the children allow him to play along so he watched them from a distance
Finally, he decided to go home and ask his adoptive parents why
That's when they asked him, "Tell us what really makes you cry?"
The little boy said, "Because the other children always tease me!"
He continued saying, "Why are they so cruel and they won't let me be me?"
The little boy's parents asked, "What do these mean children tease you about?"
That's when the child responded, "I bet you've wondered why I always scream and shout!
They always scream, 'YOU'RE ADOPTED! Where are your real parents hiding out?'
That's when I get angry and tell everyone to just get away"
The parents sat the child down and said, "Please don't be sad
They tease you because you're special, you're the child their parents wished they had"
His parents explained, "You should never be upset because you're the special one
Most parents pray for a daughter while others wish for a healthy son
You my child are special, because you were chosen
How many of these children, can say their parents chose them?
You go back to these children and make sure they can all hear your voice
You should scream out proudly, 'I'm special because my parents had a choice'
Tell them, 'Yes, I'M ADOPTED, and my parents chose me
While your parents will always wonder how you came to be
Your parents are stuck with you and they just got you by a roll of heaven's dice
So, think about that the next time that you all choose not to be so nice!'"

You Just Never Know!

Today I saw a show about a child and his dad
The son grew to a man, he met the father he never had
This child grew to become the man that he was meant to be
Yet, his hurt and anger grew inside for the loss of his own family
Until one day the man approached his mother for some answers
That's when she revealed the truth about his father's unknown cancer
All his life he felt alone because of the father he never knew
Until his mother saw his potential in what he was able to do
This little boy excelled in many ways and became quite a gifted young man
While so many others sang him praise, it was the fire inside she couldn't understand
The son that she raised had a light within him called the Holy Spirit
Each time he felt an emptiness, was another moment he could feel it
His father would call out to him and guide him to his light
Whoever would challenge the man had better be ready for a fight?
This boy appeared so happy, but never could understand why he felt so all alone
Until one day his mother would call out to him and say, "It's time to answer the phone"
I am here my son; I've watched you from my own seat
While I reside in heaven, it's your spirit that I would love to meet
Your mother has done a splendid job and raised you to be a good man
Each day is a blessing and I really need you to begin to understand
Our time together was cut short, and I'm sorry you were left alone
But the Lord called on me, as He trusted you would be fine on your own
I'm sorry that I couldn't be there, but he told me that I had to go
While I hoped to live forever, the truth is you just never know!

What My Heart Needs To Do

Today I had a moment to think things out
Hopefully you will one day understand what I'm talking about
When we first met, you made my heart race
Little did I realize, how much my heart was attracted to your pretty face
So, I just allowed my feelings to grow deep inside
I became your obsession that you tried to hide
I met you on that warm sunny day
The Lord reminded my heart of my pain from yesterday
Good morning is what my heart cried out to you
Until we find our common ground, I need to know what to do
Good afternoon my dear, let's take our time to make things right
While we discover our goals, feelings, and desires that's should take us through the night
Good evening my love, did you ever think we would land here
Since we just met yesterday, let's try to address this thing called "fear"
Where are you at in your thoughts, what will it take from me?
I need your help, let's explore the feelings that can set us free
Each day that passes is another day we can grow together
We can seek out a love that can face any type of weather
Just know that I am here with my arms wide open
Please come closer because my heart is open, and I am so inclined
Do you feel my heart racing as you come closer to mine?
Just allow me in my love, I don't want to be free and it's our time
Today I looked past your pretty face to find the real you
Thanks for showing me exactly what my heart needs to do

Goodbye Yesterday

You live and breathe every single day
But you can still remember what happened yesterday
Each time you reflect you can recall a lesson from the past
Some moments were great and yet with some I continue to ask
Every step I take, there are lessons to help me not hit a brick wall
How much did you learn before you decided to call?
Let's think of yesterday, can you remember every detail of it all?
Were there moments that were special, or did you simply hope not to fall?
Yesterday made you stronger and now it's become a part of you
Today you have grown because you have learned what to do
Do you remember when you worried about what seemed impossible?
Today you are better because the Lord saw you through
Yesterday allows you to review and reflect on what happened in the past
Reminding you of important lessons as you prepare for the future at long last
So now that you have been guided toward the sunlight of a new day
The time has come for you to remember your own yesterday
Everyone goes through their pain and their own cloudy days
As you are challenged by your enemies that try to destroy your own ways
You trusted so many instead of just trusting our Lord
The Father's love is what you need, and his anger is what you cannot afford
The Lord reaches out each time to guide you toward his new day
So, take the Lord's hand and smile because it's time to say goodbye to yesterday

I Wish I Could

Have you ever taken a moment to think about yesterday?
The time you spent alone allowed you to think of what to say
Have you regretted a moment that you may have spoken unkindly?
Have you ever wished you could take back the words spoken blindly?
I wish I could have had more time to spend with you
Tell me what would be different, tell me what would we do?
Have you ever been to a funeral and experienced flashbacks of former years?
Didn't those memories touch your heart as you held back your tears?
I wish I could have thanked you for all the things you have done
Each time you showed me the many ways that we could always have some fun
Now I've lost my best friend, your smile has been taken away
Lord help me to understand why things must be this way
I wish I could continue to smile but it will be hard after losing you
Help me Lord to figure out the next step for me to do
I wish I could stop crying; I want to stop feeling this awful pain
Each time I remember our memories, that's when my eyes bring their rain
I wish I could one day thank you again for all you've shown me
You never commented on my selfish ways, but you changed my view from "Me" to "We"
I wish the Lord would allow the world to meet the person that I once knew
Everyone has a special person, for me that special one was you
I feel so lonely today because He called you home today
So many people cry for you, all I can do is kneel and pray
Today I've decided to be strong, for I know you would
My heart has been broken today, but I wish I could

Fully Equipped

Today I watched a T.V. show about jealousy
It had the foundation of love that was hidden by Thee
The show was about a household brought together by a lie
Whenever a situation came up, the question that was asked was, "Why?"
This was a family of two children, same father but different households
There lay a secret that one day the truth would have to unfold
The father was a parent in two separate households that nobody knew about
Until one day the daughter was introduced to her brother and she could only shout
"Why wasn't this situation ever revealed to us before?" she cried out
The son and the daughter grew angry and both children stormed out the front door
The son stated to his sister, "I didn't know anything about you"
She responded "I am so angry because they kept me in the dark too"
The father asked his daughter for her forgiveness
She responded, "Why would you hide all of this?"
The son was angry but loved his dad with all his heart
He asked his sister, "Should I leave, or can we have a fresh start?"
The daughter realized too much time had already passed
As she began to hug her dad because she knew her anger wouldn't last
She decided to grow up and accept her dad's new son
That's when her heart realized that love had finally won
They both hugged their dad and began to cry about their new relationship
Because on this day they became a family that is now fully equipped

I Am Worthy

Everybody should find a mirror and say to themselves," Look at me"

Stand up and yell out to the world as you question, "Am I worthy?"

Never feel ashamed of what the Lord has created

He is Our Father and it's by his grace that we are all upgraded

We all find moments when we question why he is faithful and loves us so

Trust and believe that he has placed himself in every single one of you

While you may see things in others and find yourself wishing for those things too

Know that not everyone can handle everything but know you will have your just dues

Don't envy someone else because you really don't know their story

Be careful what you ask for because not everyone will receive GOD's glory

Instead of looking upon someone else and wishing that it was you

Tap into your own inner beauty and say out loud, "I am Worthy!"

Your time may not be now, but your moment will be revealed

Trust that your path will be your own as your fate is already sealed!

Stop complaining about what others have and what you really need

Ask yourself a question, "Do I really need it or is it just my foolish greed?"

So, today I come to you and hope this message becomes crystal clear

Do you understand that not everyone who claims to love you, will become your fear?

So, dry up those tears, and yes, the truth is going to be revealed

Until you understand your purpose in The Lord's Kingdom you may never know the real deal

Stand up to the world and let everyone know this is the real you

Set the record straight by saying, "I AM WORTHY"

Where Is Your Buy In?

The question of the day was asked, "Where have you been?"
Are you ready for your path? Will you proceed to buy-in?
Did you forgive anyone you felt did you wrong?
How can you judge someone because you felt they didn't belong?
Everyone has had a moment that they have committed to sin
So why do we judge others' paths when we know where we have been
I heard you call out, "Lord, you really don't understand my pain"
That's when the Lord answered, "It's you who doesn't know my rain
Those are my tears you feel on your cloudy days
While you became someone else's judge without asking for heaven's say!
You claim to know my Word, you even tell everyone that you are truly blessed
Yet when I called on your trust in me, you failed at every test"
The Lord's voice questioned me by saying, "Where have you been?
Are you ready now to follow My Hand, are you ready to buy-in?"
Each time you called out to the Lord and asked to be forgiven
You know in your heart, your actions wouldn't change from how you are living
Did you give anybody you met today a kind word or a helping hand?
How will you prove you're ready when kindness is something you don't fully understand?
Just because you go to church and claim to worship only THEE
When you are tested by the Lord, that's when His tears say, "You have failed me again!"
Before you stand up and feel great about who you are or where you've been
Think about your own actions and ask yourself can you commit to the lords buy-in

I Remember Way Back When

Have you ever had a moment that took your breath away?
Thought about someone who was your very own yesterday
While the past is just a memory that you may try to forget
The one who went away is the person you lived to regret
When you think about a moment that would truly stop your heart
The memory of that person was a passion you couldn't stop
The love that you had for them may have started out as a friend
Now you can recall the loving moments from way back when
Everybody has someone, who once demanded their attention
We think about what could've been, but we fail to mention
That person in your life might not ever want to fully understand
How the love you once had for another became your life's new plan
We were all young once and at that time they were your only one
As time showed us the moon, a new day showed us the new sun
But sometimes comes full circle, and sometimes old folk return
The question that remains is what lesson did you learn?
Do you give them a second chance to make your past right?
Or, do you remain hurt by the memories that made you say goodnight
Some people leave your circle for their own foolish reasons
Each pain, or memory of them will hopefully only last for a season
So, when you run into an old flame who wants to be more than a friend
Think about the pain as you visit your past of way back when!

The Lord Said Let Me In!

How many people are ready to let the Lord in?
Stubborn, hardheaded folks is where the Holy Spirit will begin
Until you acknowledge that you can't be in total control
That is the real reason why you can't hear what you are told
Every kingdom only has one seat for its crowned King
Haven't you noticed that despite you being so blessed, you still don't know everything?
Humble thy self, and let the Lord's hands guide your way
Otherwise instead of moving forward, you will keep repeating the mistakes of yesterday
Take a moment to reflect, do you recognize the people left in your past?
Some seemed worthy, some were enemies, and yet their spirits just couldn't last!
While people of your past had a role to play, but they all fell short
Each time the Lord tested their role, the Lord replaced them inside His heavenly court
The Lord removed them from your life because they weren't the right one
Your path was chosen only for you toward the Lord's only son
Listen for his voice, listen to the people who carry His message from their voice
While you listen and learn from the Holy Spirit you will understand there is but one choice
How long will you keep fighting off the path chosen for you?
Why have you taken a simple task and made it such a difficult thing to do?
How can you ever learn if you continue to feel you know everything?
Humble yourself to the Lord's will, so that you can witness his blessings
Your temple within yourself is full of nothing but the selfish you!
How can the Lord ever enter your heart to show you what to do?
Before the Lord can ever enter your spirit to really begin
You will hear his voice cry out, "My children will you please let me in?"

I Had A Dream

Have you ever had a dream that appeared to be so real?
It was the memory of the dream that allowed your heart to feel
While you were having this dream, you didn't seem to want it to end
Did you think it was an angel or maybe just a loose end?
Each time you dream of someone or something and then it becomes true
Scary how the Lord works ... as the Holy Spirit comes over you
When the Lord has a calling on your blessed life
The Lord will send his angels down to make sure you know there will be no strife
While the Lord enters your dreams to give you a little taste
The vision that you experience is so powerful for you to embrace
Remember some dreams come in parts to allow you to understand
Some are so powerful, that you might seek the advice of a holy man
The Lord will come to you in the middle of any night
To shake up your thoughts or to just show you everything will be alright
When you have a dream and it's about something so unique
That's when you begin to realize the angels have given you a peek
A dream is a vision, your connection to what may be
Do you remember all your dreams, or just the ones touched by thee?
Some dreams will scare you; they may wake you up in the middle of the night
But that's when the Holy Spirit reassures you, as He reminds you it's going to be alright
Everyone has dreams, some people may just have a scare
The question will be when or how will my spirit lose its fear
As you rest tonight, you might have a vision that might appear to be so extreme
Wake up to the fact that last night you had a dream!

No Time For Silly Games

Gather around everyone because it's time to stop the silly games
What was once fun and cute, has now become a crying shame
Too many people are getting hurt by hurt feelings or rival guns
Some people seek a peaceful life while others rather live on the run
Every one of us just wants to stay alive for another day
Why is it so hard for people to just kneel and pray?
Why are the children of today feeling like they must live a life of crime?
So many people are getting killed in the streets for a nickel or a dime
When will the violence stop, when will people realize this isn't the way?
How long can this world survive with people choosing to allow the devil to play?
The devil supplies his soldiers with your weaknesses in order to control you and have his wa
While you're playing the devil's games, he has already won by telling you to betray!
You think you're in control, you really think that you can get away?
If you listen to Satan's voice let's be clear, there will be hell to pay
You continue to abuse the blessings the Lord has given to you
Didn't you realize that the Lord allowed Satan a chance to test you to see what you would d
Don't try to bargain with your Father, because you will become his shame
While the Lord shows everyone forgiveness, he doesn't have time for silly games

Wake Up And Pray

Today I received a call from an old friend
She told me she had a dream that just wouldn't end
While she laid in her bed asleep last night
The Lord spoke to her, and asked her are you ready to fight?
In her dream The Lord told her, "Tomorrow morning be awake at 5:30 am"
She questioned The Lord's command by saying, "Why? That's not a good plan"
So, 5:30 am came and went but she remained in her bed
Not obeying the Lord's command was a sign that her spirit refused to be fed
The next day the same thing and she still decided not to pray
That's when The Lord decided to punish His angel by changing her time of day
The next day came and the Lord had awakened her from her slumber
As she rose from her bed, she realized it was only 3:30 am, she thought what a bummer
"Why Lord did you awaken me, why am I up on my feet?"
The Lord answered, "Because when I required your time, you refused to get ready to meet!"
For the next 3 days the Lord awakened her at 3:30 am
That's when it finally hit her that the Lord needed her to awaken ready to fight and pray
On the following morning the Lord awakened her at 5:30 am
She got up from her bed and prayed, as her preparation would soon begin
When the Lord tells you how to spend your night or your day
Don't ask any questions, just wake up and bow your head to pray!

Can You Admit You Don't Know?

Last night the Lord came to me in my sleep
While lay in my bed, my tears rolled down my cheeks
As I began to wake up, there was a powerful voice
"Wake up my son, because you don't have a choice"
Last night The Lord spoke to me in a very powerful way
The phrase "YOU KNOW NOT WHAT YOU DO" stuck with me today
These words were so powerful because I thought I knew it all
That's when I realized why the Lord decided to make his call
"When will you allow my spirit to enter yours and take control?
How much will you go through before you listen to what you are told?
Step back and do what must be done to let the Lord in
You have shown you know not what you do, so allow the Holy Spirit to begin
There is no room for anyone or anything else when you have control
Each time the Lord attempts to enter your spirit it's your judgement that unfolds
When will you allow the Lord's grace to guide you?
How long will you fight the Lord's hands from doing what he wants to?"
Each time the Lord reaches down to show you what must be done
Those are the moments that you decided it was time for you to run
When will you admit that you really don't have a clue?
How much longer will you destroy the blessings that the Lord has for you?
You can't go on this way by walking down a path that doesn't say go
Humble your ego by telling the Lord, help me Lord because I really don't know!

Now That Isn't Right!

Have you ever felt like you really wanted to fight?
You felt the weight of the world pushing you into the night
Have you been cheated on, or felt someone just did you dead wrong?
Times became so difficult for some reason and you felt you couldn't go on
Have you noticed how some people get so many things that they don't deserve?
Didn't you curse their complaining by saying, "You have a lot of nerve"
Well, the time has come for you to get up and fight
Let's address their complaining by saying that isn't right
Who are you to complain, you never had to struggle with anything you do?
Instead of complaining, you should look at what the Lord has given you
Everyone has a cycle of good times and bad
Would you rather lose your good times to someone who never had?
While you continue to complain about what happened to you yesterday
Didn't you wake up this morning to live out another day?
Today has come for you, so that means you have another chance
Why don't you start this new day with a prayer to give yourself a new dance?
Today you started your day by complaining about going to work
There are a lot of people who don't have jobs, so tell me who is the real jerk
Instead of complaining about your life, change your words tonight
Just know that there is someone, somewhere looking at your life and saying that isn't right!

The Devil In Disguise

Today I met a lady who was watching me from a distance
While she seemed so shy, I became aware of her existence
I paid very little mind to the fact that she was observing me for attention
As the day progressed, she approached me and blurted a suggestion
She said, "Hello Sir would you mind if I offered you my friendship?"
Only then did I come to find out her intention was to interrupt my destination
She had her own agenda, and that was to ruin my future preparation
She claimed to want to get to know me better, yet I felt the need to keep my location
Slowly the Devil laid his trap and distraction plans were set in motion
I was totally unaware of how he was using this beautiful young lady to create a commotio
Her plan was to seduce me to cause me nothing but trouble
But the Lord stepped up for me and busted her own designed bubble
While she had her own plans, that I was unaware of
My friends looked out for me as they protected me from what I needed to be aware of
They called the lady out, and questioned her intentions
They warned her to back off, as they raised their angry fists, I must not fail to mention
The conversation overheard as they stepped to the lady was, "Please don't spread anymore
We have identified you as the 'Devil in disguise'."

Over-Ruled!

There was a court case today that took place in Heaven
While everyone attended on this Sunday, which counted as day seven
Each person that arrived was ushered by Thee
One by one they entered to hear the words of His ministry
An announcement played "please come to order" as they proceeded inside
People continued to enter some with their sons and daughters
The bishop began to preach a powerful message from the Lord
As the message flowed through his spirit, he turned to wipe the sweat from his brow
The bishop yelled out, "Lord we are here to complain about each and every day"
While we live the life you provide, there is something we must say
We have come to your house known as a Holy Court
To bring forth our complaints though we know we will also require your support
Lord, we're overwhelmed, and we need to set the record straight
How much will you put in our path, how heavy will you make our plate
Lord, we follow Your Word, and each day we also kneel to pray
The burdens are heavy, it's a fight and a struggle each and every day
The Lord continued to listen to what everyone in the church had to say
The people complaining were amazed when the Lord responded in that way
"You don't have a choice." The people grumbled; some felt the message was so cruel
This was the moment when they heard the bishop yell out loud, "You have been OVER-RULED!"
The crowd said, "Please forgive us Lord but why are we over-ruled?"
The crowd grew quiet as the Lord's response echoed the church: "Because I AM THEE"
The Lord's house went silent, the people knew they had angered THEE
The Lord said, "Who are you to complain, how dare you children question me!"
Suddenly, the church went dark, because on this day the people got schooled
Today the people heard the verdict about complaining, and it was over-ruled

Do You Know Me?

Now this is a question you should ask someone
Not just anybody, but anyone who just wants to have fun
When you see me, what is it that you really see?
Do you ever pay attention to what or who hangs around me?
Tell me something about what you're looking for
Are you ready to enter my personal closed door?
Do you know the real me, or have you just observed what's on my outside?
There is so much you don't know, because I allow the real me to hide
Do you know me, or have you seen me through your own eyes?
Have you allowed your eyes to create the image of me that you want as my disguise?
Do you know me, tell me what is it that you're truly looking for?
How can you trust that stranger that hides behind closed doors?
So many people don't know themselves because they choose not to peep in
Just explain to me what will happen when the real me is revealed and you see
Do you know me, because to be honest I don't know myself for sure?
Each time something happens in my own life, I chose to run out the door
Do you know me, tell me because I'm so lost and confused at times?
I ran from the Lord only to be captured by the enemy the Devil to my demise
Do you know me, tell me what I should do?
The Lord responded, "My child, don't worry because I can handle these things"
So, the next time you have a question to ask of THEE
Listen for his answer, when he responds, "Yes, but do YOU KNOW ME!"

You Promised Me

We all live our lives doing the best we can
We are troubled by the belief that we are all in God's plan
As we reach out every day to request the lord's blessings
There are times that we question his actions as we become a part of his testing
When we feel alone, or need someone to turn to
That's when the Lord reminds us about what he has promised to you
Now the Lord never promised you that your life would be easy
He often hears you cry out asking, "Why is this happening to me?"
The Lord simply asks that we trust in his word
He promised to always be there, at least that's the message we all have heard
When times were hard you would cry out for his hand
Did he ever abandon you, because you refused to follow his plan?
Do you know of anybody who ever made such a powerful promise that was true?
If you put your trust in a friend, what happens when they don't come through?
When family and friends ask how can you trust in Thee
I turn to them with a smile and say, "Because he promised me!"
When they say, "This trust you have in GOD is second to none!"
I respond by saying, "Do you know of anyone else who would sacrifice their only son?"
I ask them if they know of anyone else who could be more loving than THEE
I say, "It's faith, my trust, his track record, the word, and most of all because he promised me!"

We Got History

Last night I couldn't stop thinking about you
As I tossed and turned because there wasn't any sign of you
When the lights went off, there wasn't anyone by my side
So, the darkness allowed my feelings to run rampant and wide
Each thought that crossed my mind was all about you
While my eyes began to cry out what are we going to do
Get up, get out of this bed and answer how could you let this be
Go on and find that heart that allowed you to create great history
Everybody makes mistakes, but only you can make this situation right
The real question you must ask yourself is if she's worth the fight
When you want something so bad, that's when it really hurts
Go get the one you love; you know she set off all your alerts
As our sirens scream, the history lights flash all night
You need to swallow that pride and go make things alright
Why would you lie there in your bed crying your eyes out?
When you have the chance to get up and find out what life's about
Every moment you allow to go by without following you real heart
Will be another moment that we allow for us to be apart
So, let's move forward and get that love back so our new path can begin
When you open your eyes to see my smile, that's when you know it's a win, win
Forget about the heartache and please come back to me
We should think of all we had as we try to correct our own history

The Lord Has Chosen You

Today I sit here with tears on my face
I thought that you left behind my smile and it was going to be replaced
While I acted so sad about my long-lost friend
The Lord reminded me that he is my faithful and true friend
Each person that we meet has their own cross to bear
We seem to lose focus of why the Lord put us all here
Well I'm here to remind everyone that it's not about you
So, pull up your big boy pants because you have a lot to do
Let's start by being grateful and extend a helping hand or two
If you think you're alone, then it's clear you really need to change your view
Wipe away those tears because we don't have time to lament this is true
Just get your act together so you can be the Lord's rod for all to see and be part of his crew
Things may seem hard and it's easy to get your hopes down
You have been chosen to stand up on the Lord's solid ground
So today I need you to stand up and begin a new fight
Your heart and God's hand will be the reason for your glory tonight
Today you have been chosen, called and touched by Thee
How much more do you need before you say to the Lord, I will walk with Thee
Guide me Lord to walk around with your light in my eyes
Allow me to carry your word to anyone who needs your surprise
I accept your path my Lord and thank you for what you would have me do
Today I see your vision; have your promise as I'm sent to represent you
I say yes and embrace the thought, "The Lord has chosen you"

Hear Me!

Today I had to listen to the Lord's very commanding voice
It was the Holy Spirit within me that informed me that I don't have any choice
Each time that the voice inside me would try to speak out
Became another sad moment that the Spirit's voice would try to shout,
"Hear me, because I have a whole lot of feelings too
How long will we go on without me listening to you?
While I'm inside you, it's the Holy Spirit that doesn't get heard
Why do you ignore my voice, why do you refuse to hear my words?
Hear me, because you are without me and you need to allow my spirit in
How can you ever learn about me, when will our road begin?
Hear me, please don't just please me for this moment in time
The fact that you don't know me is the real true crime
I need for you to listen when I talk, so you can hear what I have to say
Please don't dismiss the past because its more than a lesson from yesterday
Hear me, because the time has come for you to listen to me
How long will we dance with your disobedience directed at Thee
Be careful of what you say, think before you speak something that you may be regretting
Just know I've had time to remember all the hurt that your forgetting
Hear me, because it's time that we bring this relationship to an end
You have pushed me to a point that we are better off as distant friends
Hear me, because I want to make my feelings crystal clear
You have made me realize that all I did with you is live in fear!
So today I have been awakened by the Holy Spirt and now I know I am free
You and the Holy Spirit have shown that I need you to hear me!"

I Can't Help You Anymore

Today I told a friend that I must move on
Because every time they called on me, it was the same old song
Each time they would cry out for help from their pain
It would seem like the situation never changed from what seemed insane
While this person would always allow the pain back in
Only to relive the hurt and experience the pain from within
Each time they would call out in the middle of the night
But that's when the friend would allow them to return to begin another fight
First it was a misunderstanding that would result to physical blows
The next time their fights would come to a point that nobody really knows
She would always take him back, only to be hurt once again
That's when I would get the call, because I was her only true friend
Finally, I had to make a stand and back away from it all
Even though I knew that one day she would make another call
Please come help me, can you save me from the violence of this man?
She would always forgive him, and that's something I could never understand
Until finally I had enough and told her that I was leaving out of her life's front door
This situation is too toxic, and I'm sorry but I can't help you anymore

These Are The Last Days

Hey everyone, just look around you
Pay attention to the world before it consumes you
The Lord is very angry, and he is going to destroy us all
Take notice how things are being destroyed before his final call
Why is this all happening, why are we going through our last days
Because nobody has taken the Lord seriously by forgetting to pray
The Lord has given this world so much and still we fight
Instead of realizing our mistakes, we rather be right
Storms, tornadoes, floods, fires, they are all his signs
Yet, instead of coming together, everyone would rather commit the devil's crimes
The Lord only asks that we love each other more and pray
So, tell me why we rather ignore his request each and every day
The Lord asked a question because his temper is rising very high
Why is it that people only seek the Lord when they have a problem that makes them cry?
The second question is, why do so many people turn to a world of hate?
Who is willing to admit to this decision, knowing the Lord determines their fate?
The Lord has decided, but there is still time
Who is willing to save the world before we commit the ultimate crime?
When will we realize how much the world is about to lose?
Are you children ready to change your ways before I light the final fuse?
Time is running out, and when it does you will all regret your days
So, remember this warning because these are the last days

Let's Work On Our Heart!

Today I heard a sermon that made me look inside
We play judge and jury with another person's life
Who are we to judge another without all the facts?
We forget to understand it is the Lord who always has our own back
The Lord has held us up when we are all down and seem to be out
It is the Lord who hears our pain whenever we scream, cry out or shout
Why would you begin to doubt the Lord's spoken word?
How could we ever begin to question the Lords promises that we've heard
We have failed to look within our own self
The Lord's love looks beyond our sight to acknowledge our true wealth
So, before we judge anyone, we should first know where to start
Let's seek the Lord's direction by listening to our own heart
How long will we fight our own good that we are unable to explain
We put too much effort hurting one another without thinking of the other's pain.
When will we begin to try to heal ourselves and begin to love again?
Why can't we understand that by extending our love we become everyone's brother
Learn to find peace in love as we extend it to another
As you were given, you should give back to anyone in the land
Your blessings and gifts are yours to share, so learn to give and take a stand
Hopefully you will begin learning the lessons from your past and do your part
Own your past mistakes, be open to healing, forgive so you can work on your heart

Remember God's Glory

Tonight, I had the pleasure to listen to a story
About a man who gave thanks, as he spoke of GOD'S glory
As he sat in a chair in his own special world
He opened his heart to speak of this angel of a girl
This man was at peace, and was grateful for whatever he had
As he spoke of his story, you could tell that he was glad
This man talked about how he grew up in his dad's club
Learning what he knew but he would state he wasn't anybody's sub
The man spoke about how he knew of the Lord
Yet, his life was at a point that I simply had to applaud
He met many ladies and would know right away
These ladies of the night were told to simply go away
Until one day an angel came through the club's doors
She captured this man's eyes like nobody ever did before
So, he approached her and said, "Hello, what's your name?"
He was captured by her beauty and stated, "I'm not running any game"
They talked, and quickly became friends as she announced, "My dad's a preacher"
That's when he stated, "That's okay because I will use your voice as my teacher"
She captured his eye, while she secured his open heart
She asked him, "What would you require, what would you need?"
He answered, "I have all I want because the Lord doesn't allow me to become greedy
My wife is my backbone and I have 3 children that I love
The Lord provided me his grace from a place so far above"
I thanked him for telling me of his life story
Because he was another blessing who became God's Glory

What's Your Distraction?

Now take a moment before you answer this question
The answer may change and believe me this won't be a suggestion
Your distraction may be as simple as a smile from that pretty girl
Did you ever think a simple smile from a beautiful lady could change your whole world?
This person who has entered your circle may be placed there for an unknown reason
Yet, we follow our emotions thinking it will last longer than a season
When you leave your house in the morning already knowing what you need to do
Then distraction enters your path to change your course, the one that is meant for you
Did you plan to go straight to work, did you plan to meet this new stranger
While the signs appeared before your eyes alerting that you might be in danger
Who is your distraction, who has become your warning sign?
Which path did you choose, and who has made your sight go blind?
When will you regain the control of the life that you once planned?
Will you follow your heart, or will you succumb to the devil's own plan?
Don't get upset when your path or plans meet up with a change
Did you ever stop and think that maybe your distraction was the Lord's exchange?
Please don't be disappointed when things don't seem to go your way
Maybe it wasn't meant to be or just wait and see what happens by the end of the day
What we once considered to be such a great attraction
May sometimes turn out to become the Lord's biggest distraction
When we take a moment to think back of where we were or what might have been
That should be the moment we realize it was the Lord's distraction that saved me.

My Daddy Forgot About Me!

Last night my granddaughter was crying in her sleep
So, I woke her up because it was her sadness that made her weep
She was startled when I shook her as she looked into my eyes
As her tears rolled down her face, she asked her grandpa why
"Grandpa," she said, "what did I do that was so wrong?"
She hugged her grandpa so tight, this little angel was very strong
"Grandpa, why did my daddy forget about little ole me?
Ever since he brought home my little sister, he seems to just let me be
Grandpa, why does his new girlfriend push my love aside?
Ever since she came into my daddy's life, it's me he chooses to hide
Grandpa, tell me what must I do, to get my daddy back?
While this new lady replaces my love, how can I ever compete with that?"
My granddaughter looked at me with tears rolling down her face
The love she has for her father, is a love that a grandfather could never replace
That's when I grabbed my little angel and held her so tight
Kissed her on her cheek, and told her that the Lord will make it alright
Kaylen, there will be times when things will happen that you won't understand
Your father has fallen in love with a lady who wants to keep a man
She doesn't care about you, because you're from another lady
While she denies her fears, it's her actions that make her shady
You will have to weather this storm until the Lord clears the way
Just have faith in the Lord, even when you don't understand his way
"Grandpa, please don't forget about me, please allow me to continue in your life"
Don't you ever worry about that my angel, I'm here even after you become a wife
"Thank you, grandpa, for listening to me when I have nowhere else to turn"
You're welcome my angel for sharing your heart and all your concerns

An Inside Job For You

Today I heard a message of what we need to do
The Lord has made a path that he placed inside of you
Before you can stand before the LORD on your chosen day
Be careful what you ask for when you decide to pray
Why do you tell people that you are a born-again Christian?
When you're not even sure of the path and you have no vision
How can you ever look up and call out to the powers that be?
When you never take the time to acknowledge THEE
So many sinners need to surrender while they are still alive
Otherwise they will continue to struggle up until it's time for them to arrive
When you come before the Lord in prayer and seek advice on how to prove yourself
That will be your moment when you hear GOD say, "I already know your wealth"
As we are given the vision of the path that shows what we must do
The Lord will provide us with all our needs as he walks that path along with you
While you seek the Lord's guidance in the middle of the night
That will be the time and place that his hands will guide your fight
Before you are shown the path toward what you will need
The question will be answered as to who or what you will feed
When the time arrives, you will be guided toward what you must do
Rise up my children and know that I'm always with you
Before you can spread my word, you must learn how to acknowledge THEE
How can you expect to learn the Lord's way when every time you speak it's all about *you*?
Now that you know the Holy Spirit, I hope you understand what you must do
Just know my word and you will understand the job placed inside of you

I Didn't Do This

Today I watched a movie about five innocent men
Their story happened so long ago but it's real to the end
Their story was a painful one because it's still evident and a fact in what we see today
They repeated over and over that they didn't do what the cops wanted them to say
Even as the evidence showed their innocence and proved they didn't commit this crime
The corrupt system of that day showed the world how 5 black men needed to do some time
Each day outside the courts the family and friends would protest the injustice of the police
Inside the court the only presence was the cops, the judge who wanted to lock them up
The lawyer stated these 5 black men are guilty and need to be put away
The men stood firm and repeated, "we didn't do this crime" and refused to admit to their claim
The jury came back with a guilty verdict that made every parent begin to cry
There was no evidence, no witnesses, and no proof. The 5 black men yelled out, "Why?"
These men were sent away for a crime they didn't commit. Something was definitely amiss
Only because they were in a park that night having fun, without ever understanding any of th
The real sad part is that the person who committed the crime came forward after 20 years
They lost so much time in their lives because prejudice won again without shedding a tear
People stood together with raised fists against injustice of every race, nationality and creed
While officials watched the unfairness, remember their voices when they say, "I didn't do thi
We live in a time when people refuse to stand by and voice the corruption's sting
Hopefully we won't have to witness the same unfair treatment that prejudice can bring
The law can only work if it's used to help those who have done wrong
Will we allow prejudice to win out again or will we allow love to help us become strong?
One day we will understand that until we stand together, we will all fall
So, together let's begin that walk of trust and faith so we can one day answer the call
The next time you hear someone being accused at least hear them out without dismissing
The real crime is that when we hear the voices that say "I didn't do this", we don't care to liste

Wasted Energy

Calm down everyone who always grumbles and complains
Each day you complain about something or someone is just wasted energy
You get yourself worked up, lose focus and begin to lose your way
Did you ever take a moment to think about what GOD had for you on that day?
You wake up in the morning and feel like you're in control
Have you ever considered listening to what you were told?
As you go through your day trying to simply understand
When will you begin to realize that your life is in GOD'S hands?
Each time you complain about how life should be
You have spent another moment in your life on wasted energy
Take a moment, and please be still and just think of your yesterday
I'm sure you can begin to understand that you didn't plan life that way
As you live and breathe and follow your very own path
That's when the Lord steps in to show you his very own wrath
Stop hating somebody and being jealous of a friend
Your day of blessings will come long before your faith will ever end
Take your energy and focus on what you can surely be
Otherwise you'll just become another victim of wasted energy

Your True Hurt Place

Lord, do you have a minute because I need you
Suddenly the clouds cleared when a voice questioned, "What did you do?"
Lord, I know that you are with me, yet there is always some doubt
Just as fast as the clouds cleared, that's when the voice began to shout
Lord, please don't be angry with me, just let me explain
Everyone goes through hard times when they feel life's pain
Don't talk in riddle's, just say what you want to say
You called on me to listen, so I've allowed you to speak today
The Lord became angry because I wasn't honest with my words
Instead of just being upfront, he began to question what he heard
You called on me because you thought that I wouldn't hear you today
So now that I'm here in your face, tell me what did you do or say?
I bowed my head, dropped down to my knees and grew silent with every move
That was my biggest fear because I felt the Lord disapprove
Speak up my son, I have come to hear what you have to say to me
Yet, instead of speaking clearly to me, you have chosen to stay away
Son, the most painful thing a child can do to his parent is lie
Another is to not trust his heavenly Father from which he was sent, and he cried
You called out to your father, yet now you have chosen to become silent
Remember you should never waste a moment with Me, why are you so quiet
Today you have called me out and caused tears to cover my face
Because you called on your Father without revealing your true hurt place

It's Been A Long Day

Last night when I looked to the sky
With tears on my face I asked the Lord, "Why?"
Last night while I stared at your face
With tears on my heart I felt it was you I couldn't replace
While I sat up in my bed with a thought of yesterday
That's when I realized It had been such a long day
Each day that we live is another moment to remember
While we live in the moment through every September
When we first start our days, we must go to GOD'S class and learn
Little do we realize how life will have us sometimes crash and burn
When school days are over, and you feel you want to go and play
You never think about how fast time seems to slip away
We do so many things in our lives and yet we are still GOD'S child
We grow to an adult and remember our yesterday smile
Each day that passes gives us so much to live for
Yet most of us waste away without ever opening the right door
So, let's take a moment tonight and hear what others have to say
Hopefully we will learn from today's experience as we plan another day!

I'm Sorry For Our Yesterday

Hello, please sit down and listen to me

While I have you here in my presence, I ask myself how this could be

When I think back and remember all that we have been through

Today I must set the record straight by saying I apologize to you

Now you know how I can be and understand this isn't easy

So, please take this moment to accept this apology that comes from within me

People say you never know what you have, until it is all gone

This is hard for me to say to you my confession is to admit that I was wrong

Each time that we argued, each hurt feeling that I put you through

Was just my own denial of the fact that I would refuse to accept the real you

Who does this to a real friend, how did I ever allow you to go?

Too much time has passed, too many times I put on my own show

Finally, you said I've had enough, my feelings for you have grown too thin

Yet, it wasn't until you left my side, that's when loneliness gave me her special grin

Yesterday, was a reminder of the real friend that I found in you

Today became my reality check that showed me I didn't have a clue

Yesterday, was my message of how I would lose the one who really cared and was true

Today became my slap in the face because reality set in too

So, please take a moment and accept my deepest regret

I apologize for I have no defense, but most of all I want you to know I'm sorry for our yester

What About You?

Today I had to listen to all you had to say
So, I decided to respond to our very own yesterday
Please pull up a chair; you may want to sit down
The day has finally arrived for me to put a stop to our fooling around
Please hear me out; what I need to say is very tough
While I continue to spare your feelings, it's my heart that has had enough
When you make your comments about how you really feel
Do you ever stop to consider the fact that your actions show your real deal?
Just because you make some comments about who we truly are
Do you ever realize your actions show me that you have gone too far?
What about your life, and what about all the other things that you do?
Let's take a real look at your actions; when will you acknowledge the real you?
Now, don't get offended, because today is a day that the truth came out to play
When you sit and think about this message, I pray you remember your own yesterday
One day you will thank me for letting you know what was needed to be said
While some of this message may hurt, hopefully it will put our own troubles to bed
Please understand, I'm your real friend first and these actions are what you showed me
Today I found the courage to share with you what is required for us to be
Today you heard a message that I needed to share with you out loud
Today you found out why some people are no longer in your own personal crowd
Today you found out that life isn't always about you or me
Today I have to thank you for allowing me inside your circle to set your pain free
While we all need someone in our life to remind us about the miscues that we do
Please take a moment and find a friend that you can ask, "What about you?"

Just Remember You're The Child

Do you remember when you were a child who always cried out?
When you wanted your parent's attention, all you did was scream and shout
What young parents didn't understand was that they were the people in training
Little did they realize was that your actions didn't need explaining
As you grew older, things started to become harder to demand
So, we as children got disciplined; something the children of today couldn't understand
Later, in our lives we continued to grow older only to become confused
As our parents got older, smarter, and wiser they decided to enforce their rules
What happened to crying out and getting things we wanted like back in the day
Suddenly our parents got a message from their elders stating now isn't the time to play
We tried to train our parents like we did back to the way things used to be
They became smarter, wiser, and most of all educated by someone called Thee
While you are brought up in life not knowing or praying to the Lord
Without a moment's notice we have been shown a life we cannot afford
When you became a parent, you were reminded of how your life use to be
Each time you act out, someone from your past says you remind me of me
Once we find the Lord and we begin to walk his walk with a smile
We are guided toward the light that may sometimes feel like it's over a mile
From the first time a child walks you notice his hands raised to the sky
Each step he takes brings a smile as his parents begin to cry
So, the next time you call out to your father just remember your own mile
Because today you found your true Father, just remember that you're the child

This Might Be Hard To Hear

Good morning my love, my heart, and most of all my friend
Please sit down, because I need you to accept our end
We have known each other for so many years
Yet, while you sleep soundly at night, it's me who sheds these tears
Too many people stay together for one reason or another
We continue to live our lives acting like a sister or a brother
The romance we once shared has gone away
There is no other way to express my heart, so I give you this letter today
As you read this letter accept the message with my heartfelt regret
I wrote this letter for you remembering the good times we shared that I'll never forget
We smile outside to make our family and friends think that life is okay
The time has come for us to be honest about our lost love of yesterday
Now I want us to remain friends; lets walk away with our dignity
Let's be civil, understanding, and forgiving so our spirits can truly be free
We have lived a lie of false hope, knowing our love is lost
How long should we continue to kid ourselves, knowing the hurt it has cost
While we pack our memories away and live out the rest of our blessed days
Even though we are releasing ourselves from the pain we feel inside
This won't be easy for anyone to accept, but we shall give it a try
Who are we kidding by living like we are okay when we know it's all a lie?
The most important thing for us to do is admit we shall always care
So, I decided to let you know even though this might be hard for you to hear!

You're My Secret

Hello, my sweet, you may not know how much I really need you

So today, I decided to write this message to explain what you do

Never did I ever meet someone who I would need

Yet, you have become my secret that my spirit yearns to feed

When we first met I never thought about a possible connection

Then I began to realize you were placed before me so I could reflect

First you started by changing my wrongs by making me right

Who was this person the Lord had sent to me in the middle of the night?

Little did I understand how much I would miss your special touch

While I tried to resist only to realize I needed your presence like a crutch

Hello, my secret, I need you to understand how much I've grown

So many people try to enter my heart, but your love is one that has left me alone

This path that we are on is so narrow that it really scares me so

Especially when I take a step forward toward becoming a "Me" to a "We"

Hello, my secret, you have taken my heart to a whole new level

I have lived my life for me, but you have shown me that I'm nobody's devil

Today I discovered that there is more to life than I could have ever imagined

The most frightening vision I've had is of you saying you're letting me go

Hello, my secret, please understand this message from me

Slowly your heart is tearing down my walls that have been my own security

Today I decided to put my feelings from pen to paper

To let you know how much you have turned my fears into disappearing vapors

Hello, my secret, I know that these are my own feelings that hide inside of me

Just remember these words as my commitment to you will be my own eternity

To be loved by you is a blessing I can only hope brings us no regrets

So please allow my heart to reveal to the world that you're no longer my secret

Are You Doing What Your Spirit Is Told?

Good morning ladies and Gentlemen did you learn anything from your own yesterday

If you said "no" then you should go back to sleep because you need to pray

If you answered "yes!" then you're on the road that you need to be

Because too many people are so lost behind the devil's plans for you and me

Let's start out by addressing those of us who admit they didn't learn

hile you were fast asleep, do you realize how you have allowed Satan to have his own turn?

The Lord created you; he tests you to see if you have grown

Some people learn and move forward while others stay stuck and feel all alone

How much effort will it take, how much energy will the angels have to spend on you?

Before you understand the Lord's purpose in what he has for you to do

Don't be alarmed by this message. It's for everyone who walks the earth

Our time grows short, we will all find out what is really our own true worth

Every one of us has been placed here to do God's will

Once we have completed our purpose, then we will feel the earth's chill

So, enjoy each day; learn to understand that we are all meant to be

Understand that while we live and breathe each day, it's only by the grace of Thee

You cannot disappoint the Lord, because he already knows the real you

You may feel weak at times, just understand that he already knows what you will do

Stop crying about what you've already done, stop feeling that you have lost your way

Your steps were already planned by the Lord as he guided your yesterday

When you woke up, did you say thank you; did remember to pray?

The Lord woke you up anyway because he had plans for your new day

Each day you open your eyes is another day he has touched your soul

So, go out and do God's work today. Are you doing what your spirit is told?

Are You Ready For Your Next Step?

Now let's take a moment and look back to where you've been
Some moments will make you frown, while others will cause you to grin
When you take time out and go over your past
Let's thank the Lord for the steps you were able to grasp
We struggle to climb up the steps that are placed before our path
Do you really think you could have succeeded while you faced Satan's wrath?
The only reason we're able to climb up any type of steps or stairs
Is because the Lord's lessons await us as we are made to face our fears
Our steps are ordered by our Lord in his own time and way
So, get ready to climb or take a step toward his blessing or lesson of today
Whenever you try to skip one of his steps, he will make your path repeat
Because each one of your ordered steps becomes your own class that you must keep
When you miss one of his steps or try to skip past one of his lessons
You will be brought back to relive that moment and begin to give your own confession
Each step he has prepared for you has a meaning, so pay attention to where you've been
Otherwise you will be instructed to return to that step and start all over again
So, don't rush your steps; don't skip pass where you need to be
Just remember each time you take another step that it has been ordered by Thee
When your journey is over and your secret is no longer kept
The Lord will come to ask you, are you ready for your next step?

Men Are Hurting Too!

Today I met a man on a corner drinking a beer

So, I approached him with a blessing that he needed to hear

When I said, "Have a blessed night my friend"

He revealed he wished his pain would come to an end

I reached out for his hand to give it a shake

I realized the pain that was within him, he could no longer take

So, I asked him, "Sir are you going to be okay?"

He responded, "No sir, there's a reason I drink every day!

Sir, when I was a young boy a family member abused me using me as his toy

This abuse lasted for several years so I hid my own story

But I continued to shed my tears

This abuse was something that I never could understand as a child

While other children enjoyed their own childhood, I couldn't smile

Finally, I found comfort in a bottle of wine or inside a can of beer

Never revealing my story because I was too ashamed and full of fear

Until one day I heard other men were victimized too

Yet, my own pain was so deep I didn't know what to do

All I do is drink or cry out inside my own head

My family doesn't understand why I drink, sometimes I wish I was dead

I have 5 children and a wife who watch me get drunk everyday

This pain inside my heart needed me to open up to you today

Thank you for listening." As the man hugged me with tears in his eyes

That's when I said, "Sir, when you're ready for help from the Lord just look to the skies"

There you will find hope, healing and understanding because men are hurting too!

Did Your Last Relationship Make You Shout?

Today I heard a message about what GOD has for me
The Holy Spirit filled the preacher with a message to set me free
When we meet someone for the very first time, it's scary at best
While we hesitate, or just hold back from the Lord's hidden test
Sooner or later we decide to take that scary chance
Only to find out that what we feared was our future at a glance
As we decide to allow a stranger in to understand about their story
Little do we realize that this moment would become GOD'S glory
We approach any stranger with our own hesitation
That's when we take a new step toward our next meaningful relationship
Becoming good friends can lead to becoming so much more
Other times we have regrets for allowing Mr. or Ms. Right to leave out the front door
In the Bible it clearly states man wasn't meant to be alone
Why do so many people having relationship after relationship think they are grown
We call out in pain; we feel guilt knocking at our front door
Why do we repeat the same mistakes by going back for more?
The Lord speaks to our spirit by questioning why you have returned
Didn't I close this part of your life? When will you ever learn?
The one meant for you will listen to your very own heart
They will throw their past away so you can both have a fresh start
Your new relationship will have its own problems and you will need to figure them out
Don't follow your past or you will once again scream and shout

Children, I'm Afraid

Every parent pretends to be strong all the time
We have an inner fear that commits the ultimate crime
Each parent knows they have their own personal weakness inside
Some will admit their hidden fear that won't allow them to hide
Can you turn to your child and reveal how you truly feel?
The pain in their face might come at a cost that they refuse to reveal
"Help me" is the cry that your spirit wants to say
When the strength to speak out is answered by saying not today
We are given children by the Lord's favored hand to embrace
So why is it so hard to hide the pain revealed in our face?
"Help me" is so powerful when you reveal this phrase
This is a statement you may never hear from your parent's good days
Your children are placed in your life for the Lord's reason
Some will love you all their lives while some only share for a season
Treasure your children, stand by them whenever you can
Some grow to be proud ladies, the others will become a good man
But you must trust that most children think you will always be
Whether you have pain, become sick, or just become very needy
Open up to your children and never let your connection fade
Because the day will come when you will reveal to your children that you are afraid!

Love In Numbers

Today I watched a program about how love can shine through
We seek love and hope from a chosen few
Some people look for love in all the wrong places
Only to find disappointment in their so-called friends' faces
The show revealed a young man who was shot saving a friend's life one night
He lay in the I.C.U. praying he would be alright
The doctors informed his family that his chances where very slim
He opened his eyes and told his mother that her spirit was within him
He promised he would fight to survive and return to her
The doctors had their doubts and his vision became a blur
His deceased father's memory came in flashes that gave him the will to live
They rolled him into the operating room; he asked everyone to forgive
He sent a message through the neighborhood to please stop the fight
That's when his friends gathered their friends in the middle of the night
The whole school, the neighbors, lit candles and posted signs outside his window
They all came to pray for a man, they didn't all even know
Suddenly the doctors emerged smiling from the I.C.U.
Looking for the family as they all gleamed like a child
The doctors told them that the surgery went very well
We are all very hopeful, but it's still too soon to tell
The man was finally able to stand on his own two feet
He was then asked to come to the window to witness what his eyes could greet
Approximately two hundred people had gathered from this small town in tears
Grateful to see their football hero had risen to erase their fears
They stood outside as strangers; they rose their candles high
Today in this small town, love in numbers had their miracle answered by the Lord in the sky

One Of The Lord's Miracles

Today I heard a testimony spoken by a very grateful man
He spoke of his past in his troubled land
This was a man who spoke of his life in his own way
Until he visited the doctor whom the Devil spoke through that day
The doctor told him his test had come back and there wasn't anything that could be done
So, the Lord sent his angel to inform him that the Devil was the one at play
he angel said, "Go back to the doctor and recheck your colon for cancer to avoid your end"
The Devil is a liar, and you will discover he was never your friend
When the man got his results, he was informed that the cancer had arrived again
He informed his mother of the results and she broke down and cried
His mother would only speak on his life in negativity
He had to tell her I need you to please take that spirit away from me
He turned to his Bible to learn more about the Lord
Turning to his real father, needing the hand of a higher accord
The Lord spoke to this man and told him, "You are my son
Go back to that same doctor and you will be told you are cancer free and it's done"
Today this man is so grateful and spreads the good news of how he was blessed
He felt the Holy Spirit raise him up for another test
Today this man's tears roll down his face
He sang a song of worship that brought down this holy place
Each person who heard his testimony looked up as their eyes became full
As they became another witness to one of the Lord's miracles

Hey Old Man

Today I met a young man who called me an old man
He looked me in my eyes and said, "I just don't understand
Old man, why do so many old people reflect on the past"
That's when I told this young man to sit down and learn something today
Young blood there is so much you won't understand, but I will educate you anyway
Don't think that life is so easy, because your life could end as soon as yesterday
Each day you open your eyes will be a new blessing you've been allowed to live
Learn what you can, but most of all try to learn how to forgive
Too many people find satisfaction in enjoying other people's misery
Sooner or later you will discover that there is enough hate for everyone to see
You will find family who enjoy fighting while they tear each other down
Only to lose the ones you trusted, and find they are no longer around
You will find out in life that you won't be able to win every fight
You try to understand your friends, they may become your enemy tonight
You will discover the pain of life is a lesson that will come at a cost
Just when you feel you understood life that's when you find out you are truly lost
Young blood, I'm here to tell you don't nobody get old being anybody's fool
Learn as much as you can by becoming the Lord's favorite tool
Yes, I'm old because the Lord has blessed me to see his holy light
I learned from others' mistakes by fighting the Lord's holy fight
So, while you remain a blessing to the world and live long enough to understand
Smile and give respect to anyone that has earned the title of becoming an old man
That's when the old man turned and said it's my job to teach the young
Before you judge the old young blood just know your journey has just begun
There are stories and lessons you can learn from an old man!

The Lord's Beat Down!

Last night the Lord sent a message to me
As I lay in my bed I heard the voice of THEE
So many people feel they are doing the right thing
What message are they sending; are they ready for the lord's sting?
The voice of the Lord was so loud and clear
The Lord asked, "What will you do when I show the world my fear?
When will they realize it's my love that needs to be fed?
What must I do in your life before you end up dead?
Take heed my children because I am not playing around
Remember my warnings because I'm preparing a great beat down
I will bring so much violence into your small little world
The beat down I will bring will be felt by every man, woman, boy and girl
You will see great countries fall and they will experience so much pain
I will turn your skies dark and bring my own rain
The world will cry out to me asking, 'Why have I turned my back on you?'
That will be my moment to answer, 'That is what you made me do'
I will take away your protection; you will see crime rise in your streets
Each person who crosses your path will be someone you'll be afraid to greet
No longer will your happiness be something you pray for
Your hope for survival will become just another closed door
The wrath on this world will become too scary for anyone to be around"
Some will call this Revelation. I will name it the Lord's beat down!

Sorry

Now this morning I heard a message that brought me to tears
It was so powerful that it made me face my foolish fears
The bishop asked a question that made everyone sigh
He asked, "Do you ever say sorry, and if you don't, I question why?"
Until you humble yourself and admit you were wrong
How can you come to church and sing that Christian song?
Until you deal with your denial in a Christian way
How can you sin 6 days and come to church every Sunday?
Now I know we all have faults and we fall short
Yet, you know when you're wrong, but still lie in court
The bishop yelled, "Don't say sorry if you don't mean it"
Sorry is a word that requests forgiveness so the other person can receive it
Now to humble yourself enough to admit that you are wrong
Is very powerful, indeed and it makes a weak man strong
With the word sorry comes a very strong healing
That's when you face guilt and it's the Holy Spirit, you're feeling

Be Real

Today I met a lady who told me of her past
She spoke about the lies and deceit she couldn't grasp
Her eyes filled with tears; her emotions ran so high
She could no longer hold back the tears from her eyes
Weeping she said, "I only want a man who can be honest and sincere
A man who is strong and can address me as dear
I only want someone who understands my heart
A man who will stand and lead from the very start
I only want a man who can understand the Holy Spirit
A man who will fight for the Lord when he hears it"
I turned to her and said, "I understand all of that
Yet, what have you offered, or have you turned your back?
All my life I've been a trustworthy man
Only to be hurt or deceived for reasons to this day I don't understand
Now I know, you really can't understand how I feel"
Excuse me she said, "Do you have any idea how hard it is for a man to be real?"
I turned to her and said, "Hold up, it's my turn
You are a lady and I understand you've been burned
But how can you claim every man isn't real?
You complain about your past without allowing others to deal
How many have you rejected when God sent them your way?
Only to remain safe and lonely day after day
It's your heart they have stolen and you're right on how you feel
But until you forgive, I ask, are you for real?"

Friendship

Well now people, I thought that I would mention
This message is for those who fail to pay attention
You need to realize that all that glitters isn't gold
Some call themselves your friend, be careful of what you're told
People envy you for the person you are
Yet, they are also jealous and can curse you from afar
You may think you have a friend who greets your smile
Given the chance they will stab you in your back, this might take a while
Isn't it a shame how some could hug you every day?
Yet, when your back is turned you would be surprised at what they say
Let's not forget how you have trusted the so called "friend"
When you let your guard down, that's when you realize your friendship had to end
Trust is something that you shouldn't give early, yet most of us do
Only to be disappointed as you are deceived by those so close to you
Did you really think those people had your best interest at heart?
They were your devils who wished you harm from the very start
So, learn to listen to the Holy Spirit that resides in you
Jesus is your one true friend that will show you what to do
The word "friend" is very powerful, yet we say it every day
Not realizing very few people can earn this title until we pray
So, don't be foolish, don't allow your guard to slip
Next to Jesus's name should be a sign which reads "friendship"

Doubt

Well now this is a topic that all may live
Whether we believe in a moment or refuse to forgive
Things happen to everyone, and this may cause us to doubt
We go through life hoping things will work themselves out
Doubt is a feeling that is all in our heads
Instead of our believing, our questions are fed
Doubt comes around when you have expectations
We hesitate to believe, and this leads to frustration
Doubt is something that is okay to feel
When God delivers you, that is when you feel he is real
Now don't get me wrong, doubt comes without warning
If you allow it to become comfortable, it will feel it's belonging
God has no problem with the feeling of doubt
Because that is when he steps in to show you what he is all about
In the Bible, there was a disciple named Doubting Thomas
While others had faith, Thomas stirred up a fuss like he had no promise
When word came out that Jesus had returned
Doubting Thomas needed proof, he showed concern
Jesus came to his disciples who seemed to be all in a fuss
First, he approached Doubting Thomas who needed to adjust
Jesus understood and said, "Thomas believe; there is no need to doubt"
That was the moment Thomas accepted what Jesus preached about

Let's Make A Deal

Now I have a confession to make, so let's keep it real
This isn't a game show called," Let's Make a Deal"
This is my confession of how I'd sunken to a very low place
I was lost in my life, as I reached out and met the devil's chase
I was going through so many problems and I felt I had nothing else at stake
We are always warned about the choices and decisions that we make
One night I was sitting in my bed and I called out to the devil and said, "Hey!"
I didn't hear a response, but there was something urgent I needed to say
You see, I didn't believe there was a God
If he existed, why had I been called to suffer and experience so much?
I was only a child who was lost, confused and out of touch
I didn't understand, if there was a God, why He would do this to me
Everyone I knew was living life to the fullest, just like "O'Reilly"
I called on the devil, because I knew he could bring me out of my valley
With nothing else to lose, I said, "Devil, let's make a deal
Take away my hard times and allow me a happy life to live
I'll become your helper and never allow others to forgive"
Yet, this deal that I offered never seem to be approved
My vision was changing, and my spirit was truly moved
Then my brother had come to me and said, "Let me introduce you to the Lord
He told me to change my ways and God would soon applaud
From his sick bed, he called out, "Ronnie, one day you will understand how I feel"
That day, I gave myself to God and I told the devil, "We have no deal!"

Don't Complain

Now I want you to take a moment and feel God's rain
Whether it comes down as water or comes to us as pain
This might sound strange to many people who don't understand
Who are you to criticize any woman or any man?
Many people find a reason to criticize what may seem strange
But are they ready to take on life's challenge and make the exchange?
It's easy to be just like everyone else and follow a script
What about the person who remains unique and won't follow it?
You see, when you are different and try something new, it is called insane
Most people just look and judge or find a reason to complain
I point this out to make you realize that it's not about you!
Just follow the Holy Spirit as it guides you on what to do
Don't worry if led down a path that no one would dare to go
You're unique in your walk and with God; why should you fear at all?
People will always criticize whether for or against you so answer the call
Real friends don't criticize but will support the things you do without protest
People don't realize that when God is in your life you're truly blessed
Follow the path he has laid down for you and you will pass every test
You may not understand why you're asked to do certain things, and that's okay
When God finishes with you, that's when his glory will show the way
People stand up to the world and raise your hands to the rain
You have been chosen to walk a path in faith, so please don't complain

Under Construction

Lord, can you help me, I seem to have lost my way?
As the sky opened, a voice said, "Say what you have to say"
I tried to be a person of Christ
My path has been blocked without sacrifice
I allow my greed to get the best of me
Even though I know right from wrong, I still avoid Thee
Each time I try to regroup, I find a path of destruction
My heart cries out, but my soul is under construction
The Holy Spirit came and gave my body its chill
As I thought God left me, The Holy Spirit imposed its will
When you take one step, I'll take one with you
Believe in Me, that's all I ask you to do
As you go through life, don't allow any obstruction
I know what's in your heart, you're Christian under construction
So, when you seem lost, that's when you call to Me
Look over to your left, and you will see that your spirit walks with Thee
Walk through life with Me, and watch how your life flows
Like My promise to the world, do you see My rainbows?
So, don't be shy, just understand your function
For those who seem lost, they are just Christians under construction

Ungrateful

Today I met a woman named Sherry
She was a beautiful lady whose life was a hurry
You see, this was a lady that was blessed to no end
Beauty and brains, but her life was filled with memories from way back when
The one thing she lacked was faith in the Holy Spirit
She stated she grew up in the Catholic Church, but didn't want to hear it
Sherry spoke about how she grew up being poor
Saddened by her memory, as she looked to the floor
She spoke about how she spent her childhood in the hospital
Although she didn't enjoy her life, her spirit was full, that's remarkable
As she grew older; she became a strong lady indeed
She enjoyed the Lord's blessings, but so grew her greed
Sherry spoke about how she always helped without receiving
Giving off her back, yet she had no faith in what she was believing
She continued to share about how God had let her down
This made me angry and I could no longer hold my frown
How dare you complain about how God has treated you
Did you ever review your life as you live without a clue?
You come here for help, yet all you do is complain
Instead of looking at yourself, think about who caused your pain
God looked after you, picked you up and made you whole
Instead of giving thanks, you refuse to do as you are told
Stop and think of what life has given you; hasn't God been faithful?
Beauty and brains, yet you've been simply ungrateful

A Toxic Relationship

Well hi everyone who has a special one in their life
Whether they're your lover or a potential spouse
I want you to look at that love you've found
Are they really what you need or are you just fooling around?
Did you realize when you met they carried a whip?
Always bringing drama, causing a toxic relationship
Do you have a person who is just an elevator ride?
Did they really want your loving or was it just sex and pride?
Now, a relationship is like an elevator; it has its ups and downs
Have you found your future or have you met Bozo the Clown?
Look at what they've done with the time you've invested
Do you see yourself improving or have your wits been tested?
I want you to question whether they are a refrigerator or garbage can
Have they become one of trust or someone you cannot stand?
You need to realize that your circle of friends should be small
In your time of need, will they come to answer your worried call?
So be careful who you trust; pay attention to their whip
Don't be fooled into having a toxic relationship

Mistakes

We all seem to think we've gotten everything right
Yet, when we get the results we find we are wrong like day to night
We all seem to think we walk tall and strong
But the reality is some rights are so wrong
All we need to do is sit and listen
It's the word of the Spirit that we have been missing
As we go through life we raise the stakes
Yet, humbled by His word we admit our mistakes
The Lord only requires that we live as Thee
Forgive those who hurt, Lord can this truly be?
A voice then came and spoke of the stakes
I forgive you of your sins, I forgive your mistakes
If I, the Lord, can give you a chance
Why do you feel you can't go another dance?
Uplift your heart, forgive those with a grudge
Only I am the Lord, who are you to judge?
So, the next time you feel better than another
Remember my word and just forgive your brother
For when you do this your spirit can raise the stakes
As you walk with Thee, doesn't he forgive your mistakes?

The Cage

Good Morning everyone who is within the sound of my voice
You have made your decision, but did you make the right choice?
This message heard today was powerful; it brought me to tears
It was one which spoke volumes and reminded me of my former years
Today's message might cause one to go into rage
It was a sobering reminder of how we all live in life's cage
We are all programmed from early childhood of the do's and don'ts
Each time we've tried to change, our thoughts have said "it won't"
How long will you live within the restrictions of the cage?
Will you trust our Lord and turn a new page?
How long will you be afraid to reach for a better tomorrow?
Will you continue to be a caged animal drowning in your sorrow?
Many people blame their childhood on why they live with restrictions
Yet, you are now an adult living with your own contradictions
How long will you remain locked up in your own cage?
Living a life of sadness, refusing to explore and turn to the next page
Like any animal that is locked up from birth
Never able to wander free to find their true worth
Step out from the bondage that exists in your mind
Reach for the heavens, true blessings won't be hard to find
Or you can remain confined in your sadness never turning from life's sad page
Blaming the world for your captivity in the cage

Dangerous Kiss

It started one day, a morning of bliss
Your sweet lips, a dangerous kiss
Your warm embrace, a feeling inside
A pretty smile that you could no longer hide
To wait patiently with nothing to risk
Tomorrow would come, and so would your kiss
To love you girl would be easy to do
So, keep me close, and I'll protect you
The days that become long are the ones I do miss
Your sweet embrace, your dangerous kiss
We started to hide, we'd roam the halls
To kiss, embrace, without any shame at all
Time has passed, yet we still can't miss
The loving we started with a dangerous kiss

I Must Die

I must die so our relationship can live
I must listen with reason and learn to forgive
What God brought together, let no one deny
If we want to live, then I must die
I've caused you pain with my verbal attacks
When I think of my actions I want to take them back
Instead of talking to my partner, I'd seek a friend
Always being right and never wanting to bend
What I need is focus, what I need is direction
I need your forgiveness, I need your affection
What is required is commitment without lies
So, as I look for answers I search the skies
Followed with the question I always ask, "Why?"
That's when I realized for our love to grow, I must die

An Innocent Child

Today was a day I listened like a child
So intense was her story, I could no longer smile
As she spoke of her past, her eyes held her tears
Her sadness is what she has held back all these years
We all have a past that leave us wondering
We look for relief as we look up to the sky questioning
We feel so responsible, yet helpless as a child
We could only suppress what once was a brilliant smile
Now don't feel guilty for something you had no blame
And for the adult who hurt you, they are the shame
What you didn't realize was the Lord's extended hand
That abuse you felt from either a woman or a man
It wasn't your fault, so learn to forgive the past
When you learn to live past it, the sadness won't last
Whether you smile unto others or just continue to hide
Learn to forgive and swallow your pride
The past is something that neither you nor I can change
So, give up your sadness; you'll welcome the exchange
When you came into this world you came with a smile
So, forgive your past, because you were an innocent child

I'm Sorry I Worried You

As spring approached, so did your tears
Your worst thought of all came with your close fears
I made so little time for me and you
And without thinking the results made you blue
I'm sorry my time for loving you got buried
Please forgive my foolish ways, because it's you I worried
A simple phone call or even a faithful thought
Would have saved your grief, would have saved us from court
Yes, I'm guilty of not making that loving call
That makes me guilty of causing your heart to fall
But of all the things I'm truly sorry for
It's for hurting the one I love and truly adore
See, you never know how much you really care
Until the day comes when there is no time to share
We'll sit at night and remember all our good times
We can even search the skies for our secret crimes
After all that searching after all those tears
We shall come together, and once again embrace our fears
I caused you grief; I caused you so much pain
And like the clouds, I've caused your eyes to rain
Baby, please remember love is something that's not hurried
And if you missed me, I'm sorry that you worried

Who Hurt You?

Excuse me lady, why do you seem so sad?
And why do you allow him to treat you so bad?
You say he's gone, but you still think of him
Who hurt you so bad, John, Joe or Jim?
When I look at you, I see a pretty smile
It was the one you had, ever since you were a child
Lady don't be sad; just listen to what you must do
Answer my simple question, who hurt you?
Please understand, he isn't the only one to blame
If you allow him your space then you must share the shame
Pick yourself up from the dark corner you now possess
Stand up to your past and learn how to confess
You can't change what happened, but you do know what to do
Remember my first question, who hurt you?
You should thank him because he has made you strong
So, with your new heart, give it to whom it belongs

The 5 Steps Of Passion

I've laid you down and traced your skin
I've tasted your body where my hands have been
I've licked your left thigh and sucked on your right
I've thought of our days and enjoyed our nights
I've wondered why we came to be
I've enjoyed the passion you've given me
One man's loss is another man's gain
If we lay, there shall be no pain
Prepare yourself, because the steps are sweet
I've watched you tremble and lose your feet
To lick your body and be your number one
I've watched you stutter as your body went numb
Each step we climb, we'll climb as we
Feeling your body, knowing that it needs me
-Let's Climb These Steps-
Step #1 is to enjoy your passion and style
Step #2 is to enhance your smile
Step #3, now this step will be very demanding
Step #4 is that our minds keep in touch since never has anything meant so much
Finally, Step #5 is that we obtain great trust
Since without all five, we'll only have lust

Are You My Baby OR
Have You Become My Maybe?

When I think of all we've done I call you my baby
Yet, as I look for your love you say maybe
I seek you out for your affection
That's when I notice you're in a different direction
So, I must ask when will we become one?
Or have we grown away from love and only seek some fun
Why do I feel you slowly slipping away?
Instead of coming for my love you tell me not today
How long will we run away from what we started?
What once was lust, seems to have departed
Have you lost interest in the passion that we shared?
Why does it feel our love has become just people who care?
You once stared in my eyes and I felt your heart
Now we have only memories while we grow further apart
To think of you made me want no other
Time has caused us to act like a sister or a brother
To love someone and be in love are two different streets
What we had and what we have makes me afraid – wonder if we've peaked
I'm not blaming you, but I want you to be honest with me
Are you my baby or have you become my maybe?

The Good, The Bad And The Ugly

Today we heard a message that went very deep
We sat to listen; it was the spirit we'd keep
The question was asked about who we are
When the bishop yelled out, his voice carried so far
Which person are you showing to the world?
As he spoke with command his words hurled
Are you feeling as though you are in a very good place?
Meanwhile you hide your thoughts that show on your face
Or are you that bad one that all should fear?
You act so well; many believe you care
Are you the ugly one that is just nasty to all?
Making everyone wonder when the devil will call
You live your life playing all these roles
Listen to the Spirit and do as you are told
Because everyone fits the stranger description
Feeling you're always right and acting like you're a true Christian
Well, the Lord knows you from inside your heart
Listen to the words that help you play your part
There will always be times that you will ask how could I be?
The good, the bad and yes even the ugly

A Strange Desire

I woke up this morning with my heart on fire
Craving for your love, feeling a strong desire
While I think of the time, I spend with you
My feelings draw a line of what I can do
Desire is felt for the things out of reach
Yet, I want more of your fruit that I call my peach
I toss and turn in the middle of the night
My strange desire informs me, things will be all right
No matter what happens, I feel your belonging
To my heart and my soul as I wait for the morning
You sleep at night in another bed
My hunger for your love remains unfed
So, I lay down at night with my burning fire
Hoping to understand this very strange desire
Many have loved and felt heartache and pain
So, why does my heart cry out for your loving rain?
Each time that I reach out to feel your embrace
Is a time I hope to see your pretty face
I only hope that one day my heart understands your fire
So, that I will understand this strange desire

Do You Know Needy OR Greedy?

Well this is a question that we all know
Some are so transparent while others never show
Sooner or later they will show up in your life
Whether they are a friend, a husband or a wife
Now, the person might tell you all the right stuff
When you get caught up in their web you never get enough
Yet, because you got caught in their "Web of Lies"
You became their victim when you finally realized
They might love you for what you can do
While others will show that they really don't care about you
They always have their hand out for some kind of need
And that's when you realize the hand that you feed
Needy is someone who has a need all the time
Yet, you feel guilty as they continue to blow your mind
While you want to say no, you feel that they are what you need
As you are drawn closer to their own personal greed
More and more they will take all that you own
Until you get fed up and tell them to leave you alone
So, be careful of the person that you meet today
Or you may be the next victim of greed's prey

Listen

There are times in our lives we move Heaven and Earth
No matter the situation – WE NEVER GET WHAT WE'RE WORTH
But never in life did I dream of us two
So, it's me who give thanks to the Lord for you
-I 'm Listening-
We met early one morning through the glimpse of the eyes
Your beauty was stunning, and that is no lie
Single, alone this surely can't be
But the question still came, did you have time for me?
-Still Listening-
As our hearts raced, and temperatures would rise
You invited me out, and that too was a surprise
We talked of our past, we laughed out as one
Never did we dream of each other having fun
-Just Listen-
So now my dear Lord, I give thanks for this girl
Most men search their whole life, they search the whole world
I have listened to rumors, I have listened to friends
But now it's time for me to put all of them to an end
Ears are for listening and I have done my part
But the feelings I've grown, because I've listened to my heart
So, give up on your sweetheart, you don't know the real me
I keep what I want, and this you shall see
We have waited so long to put trust into love
So, listen to His voice He's our Father above

Where Is she?

Do you remember when you really cared?
Your heart would race to the one with whom it was shared
As time passed you would give him your all
Each passing moment would cause your emotions to call
When we meet, you shared how your feelings were deceived
Thinking your love would be returned when it was received
Now time has passed, and you carry hurt in your head
What once was love and affection has now been labeled dead
Why would you allow another person to change the real you?
Knowing you have so much love inside
Yet you fail to do what you need to do
While you go home at night with a smile on your face
Instead of happiness you've allowed emptiness to take love's place
You once told me that what hurts you will make you strong
Yet, you allowed another man to kill your sweet song
You once told me you would enjoy giving a man your pleasure
Now, due to the hurt they have buried your loving treasure
You prayed last night; you asked the Lord for the one
He has answered your request by sending you his son
So, please pay attention when you're told of a need
You're responsible to keep him happy and his desire is what you must feed
Because you've been lost, living life like you can't see
I've been looking for the girl as I wonder, where is she?

Suppose

The Lord asked a question that should shake you up
The question was so powerful it would make your heart stop
The question he asked might make you tremble
While you think of an answer, it was fear you would resemble
He asked everyone as they awakened from their slumber
Suppose you were asked; would you sacrifice your son would you stumble?
Think about that question, because I have many to ask
Suppose you didn't have what I was given, you could handle each task
As you wake up and you're able to rise to your feet
Suppose I was like you, would I be someone you would like to meet?
What if you only had one day to live?
Suppose you met your worst enemy, would you be able to forgive?
Each person that crossed your path did so for a reason
Suppose you didn't know them; would you have learned from the season?
When I gave you a look as the real person in you
Suppose I didn't come to show you my rescue?
How often have you judged someone without reason at all?
Suppose I became you and allowed you to slip and fall?
Have you become ugly to a stranger you never met?
Suppose I showed you the path that you would live to regret?
So, the next time you meet someone and turn up your nose
Just ponder these thoughts when you meet suppose

Be Happy For Me

Hello everyone, who has tears in their eyes
I am here with our Father just look to the skies
While you seem at a loss on this happy day
Please listen to my voice because I have something to say
Today is a day that we should all reminisce
Just think of our good times, think of the times you will miss
Instead of the phrase, "Lord how could this be?"
Just keep up my memory and be happy for me
Now I've left your side, I've left your close space
I've left your world, I've left tears on your face
Our Father has welcomed me home in His arms
Calling His angels, setting off all kinds of alarms
The gates have been opened to welcome me here today
My spirit is alive, and I've found comfort in a heavenly way
So, for all my family and for all my friends
There is a heavenly gate where I thought was the end
I want to thank all of you, please understand I am free
So, don't cry, don't be sad, just be happy for me

Kiss-Kiss

Hello Lady, now I want you to reminisce
Can you think back to our first kiss-kiss?
Now, this is something that is unique
As your mind wonders, it's your lips that want to speak
Now, we may be apart at this particular time
Just know that no matter where you are, you are still mine
While you are away from my strong arms
I hear your spirit calling out with all types of alarms
When we are not together it's your smile that I miss
My heart beats fast as my thoughts remember our kiss-kiss
I'm sorry that time just continues to run away
I miss you each night, I look for you each day
We have allowed our feelings to grow to new heights
When we argue, those are just love moments for another night
Each day that we don't have each other to enjoy
Is a day of sadness, Baby know I'm not your toy!
So please don't play with me, I need your fire
Come back with your heart and I'll become your desire
Let's not waste time, let's make sure we got it right
I've waited for you all my life and now I want you tonight
So darling, now that you know you're the one I miss
Come closer to my heart so my body can give you a kiss-kiss

A Love With Restrictions

Why does love to have any restrictions at all?
If you truly love, then you've made the ultimate call
Those three words don't ever come cheap
It is trust, commitment and honesty that you keep
There are some who claim they are in love .... "but"
Now this is a statement that makes me erupt
Don't say you love someone but there is a limit
Why would you hesitate if you're already in it?
How can you "love" someone and make this conviction
When you love always has some restriction
Why do you feel you can say these precious words?
If you break it down, the meaning becomes absurd
To say the words, "Honey, I love you but not tonight"
Is a slap in the face which could lead to a fight
Now if one is sick or not feeling well...
Then that's understood because your desire may have fell
But when you love someone and can't show affection
How long do you think you will keep them in your direction?
No matter what your excuse is, they will soon grow annoyed
That's when they feel rejected and the devil is deployed
People's minds wander when they are angry or disappointed
This doesn't mean they've lost the love you appointed
Needs come with everyone and you will need to accommodate
Some will wait for a while before some other person steps to the plate
Now don't get me wrong this doesn't change how I feel
The heart knows what it wants, but lust will try to steal
So, pay attention when you're requested to deliver
The heart is on notice while the spine starts to shiver
Don't say no to my desires, please not tonight
You can't love with restrictions, it only leads to a fight

A Dangerous Love Ride

What seems so close can be so far
The time we spend goes faster every day
But to give it back is not even a thought
To stop seeing my love they would need the "People's Court!"
I've come a long way and there's no turning back
What seems lost and confused, is now right on track
So, don't second guess or question the decisions I've made
Don't offer me anything because I am not willing to fade
Just leave me with this decision made for me
Go on with your life and please let me be
My heart is filled, and can't take no more
So, don't question me as you walk out the door
Just be happy for me, I found peace of mind
To come home to an empty house, just to unwind
To embrace the pain that was given to me
So, you can't be happy for us, then let me be
Thank you for the distance that you've given me
So, we may go on and take another run
Only to have and to hold our love that once was fun
But if we remain true, sincere and respect each other
Then it's our love that won't allow another

Are You Loving A Liar?

Now this is not any kind of question
This is a reality check that needs to be mentioned
The love that you have, is it for real?
Because love brings pain; are you ready to deal?
When you first met the person of your dreams
They were the one…or so it would seem
So, you gave them some time to get to know you
Is this something that you usually do?
As they come into your heart and soul
Did you believe the story that you were told?
It's easy to listen while you see the lies
Yet love hides the heart with deception in its eyes
Now, you have let your guard down for your heart
The liar has arrived with the deception from the start
The handsome man or the pretty young girl
Has come to you promising a fantasy world
Yet you allowed them in because you trusted
Are you starting to realize that your heart is busted?
As time passes by, you start to see signs
When will you pay attention to your lover's crimes?
Are they guilty of having love with another?
Only loving you when they can find no other
Have they promised you the world but given you grief?
Lie after lie without any love or relief
You can do badly without any help
Can you count on your love when you make the call?
Will you get a response or are you loving a liar?

Denial

Are you ready to face who you really are?
How long before you realize you've gone too far?
The most frightening picture is the one of you
How much are you willing to change what you do?
When you look around to judge everyone but "Me"
How long will you refuse to blame the powers that be
Of course, we can always look the other way
Yet denial will always return to our present day
Don't you know that when we judge others that it is a sin?
When will we face our own demons so we can win?
The time has arrived for us to face the here and now
We need to face our fears and we will be able to say wow!
Once we come to realize and deal with our own spirit
That will be the moment we will no longer fear it
Denial is only ours to own because it means fear
The question is, "Are you ready or do you refuse to hear?"
Denial is only as strong as we allow it to be
Trust and faith come from the Spirit of Thee
So, stand up and face it because you're not a child
Today I am God's warrior and I challenge my own denial

Was It Worth It?

What happened; what were you thinking?
Or perhaps, were you high or maybe you were drinking?
Things seem so happy, so exciting with us
Now you went and hurt me and destroyed all my trust
Yeah, I know you're sorry; this may be small to you
But you lied and this is something I can't do!!
Remember how you preached the words, "I Don't lie"
I made myself believe this, now I can only cry
You went out with only you in mind to trust
But did you forget there are two letters in the word "us"
Selfish – you would go and do what you did
You knew my feelings; you know I would forbid!
But you were you, and yes, you are grown
What else will you do when you're all alone
I must wonder, where do we stand?
The girl I loved said, "I was her only man"
Yet you did this; you did it for you
Does this mean that I should do this déjà vu?
I only wonder what happened to your word
Lost was your heart because I wasn't heard
Yes, I still love but I'm hurt and must heal
The scare you put me through doesn't seem real
I must stop now to take a second look
My trust, my love, it's my heart that you took
So as long as we're together, please give it some thought
The hurt you have given me has left me so distraught
I hope it was worth it to you, all that you received
Your love that you promised me was what I believed
Yes, I'll forgive you, that will come in due time
Forget, I cannot do, this hurt will take time
But forgetting this pain would be the real crime

Pain

Now I want you to think about the real you
Not the person whom you show, while others don't have a clue
You know that person who cries in the middle of the night
Then comes back to the world, to claim everything is all right
Everyone has a secret door they want to keep closed
Never to be revealed, not ever wanting their pain to be exposed
While God uses clouds to cover His skies
We sometimes use tears to show pain through our eyes
Some become weak in the knees or start to tremble
While others try to hide the pain they resemble
Pain comes in different ways, yet it doesn't come cheap
Some try to handle it; pain can make a strong man weak
We are sometimes given pain to show that we can be humbled
It's a sign of weakness, yet it can make a strong voice mumble
Pain can come without warning, yet strike through the heart
It is a reminder we should remember to always do our part
So, whenever you feel the signs of any type of pain
It's usually because you've ignored the clouds before the rain
So, please pain attention, because pain in life is guaranteed
One day you will understand, it's pain that teaches you what you had

It's Not What It Looks Like

How often have your eyes shown your deceit?
Whether it was within your sight or a vision you would meet
How many times have your eyes allowed you to be wrong?
Whether you really believed your eyes, or your feelings were that strong
How often have you decided based on sight?
Only to be wrong, and this destroyed your night
There was a time that Jesus spoke to a lady by a well
When he asked her for a drink, it became her story to tell
She was a lady who wasn't permitted to give to Jesus in her day
So, she asked him why he would ask her this way
Jesus told her, "I am the real well, and with Me you will never Thirst"
Puzzled by his statement, she thought that he was cursed
Jesus told her, "I am the well that gives eternally"
The lady looked at him and questioned, "how can that be?"
Jesus told her, "You look at me and judge me, yet you still thirst"
The lady who grew tired told Jesus, "I will feed you first"
That was the day the lady at the well passed her test
She became full of Jesus and her thirst was laid to rest
We must learn to trust each other, whether it is Sue or Mike
Trust is so revealing because it's not what it looks like

Family

Now pull up a chair and please sit down
The word family carries a meaning that doesn't fool around
Family is a word spoken every day
Do people really feel the expression that isn't shown in any way?
Let's take a moment to examine what is shown
Are people in contact with family members, or left all alone?
Do you see your family only on happy or sad occasions?
When are you seen by family, do you need asking or persuasion?
Family is not something or someone that you choose
Family are there to be loved, not your crutch to only use
Now you must accept family, because they come with life
They are not your choice like a husband or wife
Now, you will have moments when family can be embarrassing
Yet, there will always be family who might be everything
The question is how do you fit in their circle or their tree?
Are you the root that makes them strong or a leaf that falls free?
Because no matter how you size it up, you can trust me
You will always have a moment that requires family

Discourage

Hello! My name is Discourage; do you know me?
I'm not your friend, I am the one who causes doubt in Thee
Now I hope you don't think I come cheap
You've allowed me into your life to cause you to weep
Hello! Are you aware that I am here to cause you pain?
Like any cloudy day, you should prepare for the rain
Now I know many of you feel that you can live without me
Every time you become depressed, that is when you fail to see
Do you know my purpose, do you understand why I exist?
How many times have you tempted fate by taking a simple risk?
When you were told that you didn't have the courage
You allowed me in, you know my purpose and I am here to discourage
When will you ever have enough faith to look beyond your tears?
Do you really trust your God, or will you trust your fears?
My name is Discourage, and I am here to lead you astray
Are you willing to follow me by forgetting your God today?
I only come at your sad moments when you are depressed
My job is to make sure that you fail the test

Mean Daddy

Now I heard this term used by my granddaughter
So, I had to listen, and I think all daddies ought to
Why my granddaughter, who is only two years old
Would say such a thing, or was this what she was told?
So, I asked her, "Kaylin, how on earth could this be?
Why do you call your father a mean daddy?
She dropped her head and said, "Grandpa he doesn't allow me to go very far
My mean daddy won't let me eat candy at all
When I climb on the furniture, it's his voice that calls
My mean daddy doesn't allow me to run all over the place
While other children yell and scream, he keeps me in his space
My mean daddy only allows me to run and play
Just as long as I listen to what he has to say
My daddy takes care of me and loves me very much
But when I'm home with him, all I hear is 'don't touch!'
Now, I'm only two, but I will soon be three
How long will my daddy be so mean to me?"
I lifted my granddaughter, and placed her on my lap
Smiled and said, "You will appreciate all that
A lot of little girls wish they could be
Home with the one you call, 'Mean Daddy!'"

What If I?

The question came from the powers that be
While we ask for the world, we always question Thee
Well, today the Lord asked a question of us
Do you really listen, do you really trust?
You always know my name in your troubled days
Yet, you wonder why I give you a reason to pray
The Lord asked a question, "What if I?"
Before you answer, will you look to the sky?
What if I granted you every single wish?
Would you be grateful, or would you change your focus?
What if I became a God who acted like you?
Would you be as forgiving, or would you even know what I do?
What if I made the whole world peaceful?
Would you pray to me, or would you forget my grill?
You see, the Lord must give us troubles and fears
These are the only times we seek his listening ears
While we weather our seasons, and we prepare for our storm
Would we seek him if our lives ever changed their form?
What if I gave you all that you've asked?
Would you study to learn if life wasn't a task?
What if I gave you the path to your glory?
Would you learn without a lesson; would you remember your story?
So, today the Lord sits in his heaven, in the sky
Asking all of us the question, "What if I?"

Tomorrow

Good Morning everyone who has awakened
Be blessed and know your spirit wasn't taken
While you come to the Lord only on your bad days
Can you really justify the reason that you don't pray?
Everyone will face their own moment of sorrow
So why do you feel you can wait for tomorrow?
You want your life to be blessed in every way
Yet, it's your decision that you don't kneel and pray
The Lord waits for you to come to his light
So, why do you feel that you are always going to be alright?
When you are given your moments to feel your sorrow
They are your reminders that you shouldn't wait for tomorrow
Come to the Lord and accept him today
Humble your heart and learn that he is the only way
Many have no problem when they can sing a happy song
Who really listens if you don't know where you belong?
Come to the Lord and let him heal your sorrow
Because my friends you were never promised another tomorrow

Grandpa

Now this is a title that might make you faint
From any child who calls you grandpa, you are their saint
You see, this simple word isn't really simple at all
While parents are to blame, grandpa cannot fall
Now I always said, "I don't want any more children of my own"
Little did I realize that the Lord had other plans for my home
Your grandchildren reflect their parent's own action
So, if your children are like you, you'll reap the satisfaction
My son gave me a blessing without even understanding his call
While we were so apart, we weren't apart at all
The child that he fathered is an innocent little girl
Yet, she gave life to her grandpa with a beautiful new world
Now, it is easy to say don't spoil her, be careful she doesn't fall
So, why when she has a need, it's grandpa whom she'll call?
While I am hard on my son's way, I still give him praise
The little girl that he fathered has blessed my old days
Grandchildren, I am told, are a blessing from Thee
Well, I am here to tell you, I am here when she calls out to me
Now, don't get me wrong, I am strict if she goes far
If you ask Kaylin who I am, she will tell you that's my grandpa

What's Your Relationship?

Now this message was short, but powerful indeed
It was one that spoke volumes: it was the soul it would feed
The bishop asked, "What's your relationship to Thee?"
You must find a mirror, and please don't blame me
The Lord told all of us that we shouldn't allow fear to be
"If you believe in Me, then you should listen to hear"
When you become close to Jesus, with your relationship
That's when you know that you're on a special script
People around you will change
Some will go away knowing you're different
Because you have seen a new day
When your relationship with Jesus brings you out of your norm
You will be a stronger person who weathers any storm
When your relationship with Jesus starts to draw power
You will walk like a king, and be ready at any hour
When your relationship with Jesus makes you think outside the box
You will be like a drug addict who has finished detox
When your relationship with Jesus makes you crave only Him
You will follow his voice even when you must go out on a limb
So, when someone asks, "What's your relationship with the Lord?"
Answer, "He is my savior and life without him I cannot afford"

Are You Guilty?

Now everyone should think about the question at hand
Are you guilty of anything you just don't understand?
I want you to really take a moment to think
Are you worried or confused, or are your troubles at the brink?
If you are a victim of your own troubled past
Did you think you would forget, how long did that last?
Are you guilty of going through every day without concern?
How long before your past would cause you to burn?
Are you guilty of taking advantage of how you live?
No concerns for anyone but yourself, yet now you want to forgive
Are you guilty of waking up and going on with every day?
No cares for anyone else, because you feel life should be that way
Are you guilty of being selfish to strangers you meet?
Do you feel you will always land on your feet?
Are you guilty of just feeling you live alone in this world?
Feeling you are owed by every man, woman, boy or girl?
Has it ever occurred to you that you are living on borrowed time?
Too selfish to realize this is one serious crime
Yet the day will come when you'll be judged by Thee
So, answer my question, "Are you Guilty?"

What Are You Seeking?

Hello everyone, I want you to listen up

The question of the day hit home as the crowd began to erupt

People came from all over and poured into the church today

Many came to hear the message, while others just came to pray

The question the bishop asked, made you stop and think

While some jaws dropped, others' eyes began to blink

I present the same question to you, and I will expand

Do you seek the Lord's face, or do you only seek his hand?

Now, you may ask the question, "What is the difference, I don't understand?"

One symbolizes the person, the other symbolizes your greed

When you seek the Lord's face, then you're seeking Thee

But if you're seeking his hand, then you're only out seeking your desires

It's not wrong to want or not want your wells to expire

But realize he knows your needs and knows what is required

Don't you know he caused the fires?

If all you do is come to him with your hands out seeking more

You'll soon begin to understand why you're constantly hitting the floor?

God allows you to fall, to teach you what you must learn

So, seek his face to understand his heart, or my friend, you will burn

The path you're on is where he's placed your steps, to receive his grace

Stop seeking his hands, so you can begin to seek his face

It's Complicated

Good morning everyone whose life is complicated
Do you realize how your steps have been illustrated?
We are all tested when we least expect it
Can the Lord trust your faith when you are frustrated?
Now, it's easy for you to believe when things are okay
Then the devil comes by to interrupt your blessed day
It's not that God has abandoned you in your time of need
There will be times when the devil will show you his greed
Now, God wants to know, are you only his in the good times?
When drama arises, do you become a baby singing nursery rhymes?
We are all guilty of wearing frustration, at some point in our life
Are you ready to stand tall or cut God off with a knife?
Life becomes confusing when you feel you're living life right
And along comes Satan to let you know you must fight
Why are things always a challenge; why are there bumps in the road?
These are the Lord's lessons to see if you'll change your mode
The bishop yelled, "It's easy to smile when things seem okay
But when they become complicated, are you strong enough to stay?"

Love Doesn't Have Loopholes

Good evening everyone, we have a message of love
Spoken from the heart and delivered from above
We heard an explanation of love and its true meaning
Explained to perfection as we sat with our faces gleaming
The bishop yelled out, "Are you a selfish person to everyone?
Yes, I am asking you, the one who takes others' feelings for fun"
He yelled, "Do you have excuses why you can't show your heart?
Sounds like you should have been honest from the very start"
Are you a person who always looks for a loophole in life?
You know it's the excuses, why you don't have a husband or wife
Too many people want the benefits but refuse to do the work
Do you want a free ride thinking everyone is your jerk?
The word "loophole" is another way of finding an exit plan
That is what good lawyers use when defending a guilty man
So, if you really want love, or have real love to be felt
Don't settle for my excuses, pay attention to the cards you are dealt
Love is a beautiful feeling when it is given and received
Love doesn't have loopholes; it is a feeling that is truly believed!

Hate

Attention everyone, there is a big problem at large
It is the most common problem and it starts with who's in charge
This problem is created within our parents and friends of us all
We forget about our frightful call
We all have prejudices that we fail to acknowledge inside
Now, this is the spirit that not all of us can hide
Whether you are black, white or other, you can still have this spirit
Do you choose to feed this anger, I know you hear it?
Now let's be clear, hate is fueled by ignorance and fear
It's the hate for another person, because of the skin they wear
Now you may not act out to show others your hate
Until the fatal line is crossed and this spirit changes your fate
Hate is not something you are born to do
With passing time, hate can consume you
Things may happen on your path as you live
Angered by a moment, you feel you can't forgive
Control over this spirit that was planted inside of you
May take education and understanding, just to name a few
Please take a note of what's happening in this world
It's time to learn forgiveness that's a call to every man, woman, boy and girl
Until we address our own feelings and regulate
We will always welcome the devil who teaches hate!

Lightning Source UK Ltd.
Milton Keynes UK
UKHW040017060620
364507UK00001B/238